TRINITARIAN CHRISTOLOGY

The Power That Sets Us Free

Michael L. Cook, SJ

Paulist Press
New York / Mahwah, NJ

Cover and book design by Lynn Else

Library of Congress Cataloging-in-Publication Data

Cook, Michael L. (Michael LaVelle), 1936–
    Trinitarian Christology : the power that sets us free / Michael L. Cook.
    p. cm.
    Includes bibliographical references.
    ISBN 978-0-8091-4657-4 (alk. paper)
    1. Jesus Christ—Person and offices. 2. Trinity. 3. Catholic Church—Doctrines.
I. Title.
    BT203.C667 2010
    232′.8—dc22
                                                                            2009046436

Published by Paulist Press
997 Macarthur Boulevard
Mahwah, New Jersey 07430

www.paulistpress.com

Printed and bound in the
United States of America

Table of Contents

For all my colleagues in the field of theology,
especially for the members of the
Religious Studies Department at Gonzaga University
and for the members of the Catholic Theological Society of America.
May we always be enablers of a deeper understanding
of faith and promoters of a resolute commitment
to the transformation of our social world.

Introduction

"WE BELIEVE IN THE ONLY SON OF GOD"

Paul's prayer in the Letter to the Ephesians (3:14–19), literally translated here,[1] is a powerful expression of the trinitarian life of God (to the Father through the Spirit in Christ) in its effect upon us as the Church, the body of Christ, filled with the fullness of God (see 1:22–23).[2]

> v.14 "For this reason I bow my knees before the Father,
>
> v.15 from whom every family (*patria*) in the heavens and on earth is named,
>
> v.16 in order that (*hina*) he may give you according to the wealth of his *glory* to be strengthened in *power* through his Spirit in the inner human being,
>
> v.17 that Christ dwell through faith in your hearts, rooted and grounded in love,
>
> v.18 in order that (*hina*) you may be strengthened to comprehend with all the saints what is the *breadth* and *length* and *height* and *depth*,
>
> v.19 and to know the love of Christ surpassing knowledge, in order that (*hina*) you may be filled into (*eis*) *all the fullness of God*."

The Letter to the Ephesians is a prime example of biblical testimony to the triune life of God as experienced within the Christian community. Yet its intent is cosmic in scope. It is a question of the intention or purpose of God (1:9, *to mysterion tou thelēmatos autou*) for the economy of the fullness (*plērōma*) of the times when all things (*ta panta*) will be brought to completion united in Christ, things in the heavens and things on earth (1:10).[3] Whatever the original background for the understanding of the universe may have been (a mythic restoration of the original order in a fallen universe?), there are key images here that are open to fresh interpretation in the light of contemporary views of an emergent universe.

I suggest three, following the order of each of the *hina* clauses: (1) glory and power; (2) the breadth and length and height and depth; (3) all the fullness of God. First, God's glory and power course throughout the letter and frequently issue in a doxology ("Let us praise his glory!" as at 1:6, 12, 14; 3:20–21). The glory and power of God are manifest (revealed) in the divine deeds, especially the grace of being chosen in Christ to be sons and daughters of God through faith and love and the gift of the Spirit as the seal and guarantee of the promise (1:13–14; 4:30, which includes the exhortation: "do not grieve the Holy Spirit of God!"). Doxology is the praise of God on the basis of the divine deeds or actions. Here we meet the limits of human language in the ecstatic bursting forth of praise and adoration. Jürgen Moltmann proposes that it is in such ecstatic experiences that we have access to the inner-trinitarian relatedness of Father, Son, and Spirit. "Do not all our attempts to explore even the 'depth of the Godhead' remain fettered by our earthly existence and the limits of our experience? But what then actually happens when we forget ourselves and in doxological ecstasy praise and glorify the triune God, not for our sake, but for his own sake? Are we then not departing from his operations on us and our experiences of his energies and adoring the goodness and beauty of his essential nature? What we revere for itself, rests for us in itself and exists in itself even without us."[4] The Letter to the Ephesians would agree. However much emphasis we place on God's actions on our behalf (1:3–6, God has graced us with every spiritual blessing in his beloved Son), our hope is that we be filled with the fullness of the one who fills all things everywhere (1:23; 4:10, 13).[5] How are we to understand "all things" (*ta panta*) and "all the fullness" (*pan to plērōma*) of God?

The second *hina* clause speaks of the breadth and length and height and depth. The author tends to stress spatial imagery more than temporal (but he does have both: see 1:21; 2:7; 3:21; 4:12–13 for references to time). Again the background, though found in many possible sources, is vague and the intent is more rhetorical. "What he intends the words and symbols to mean can be deduced from the context: The Mystery of Salvation revealed by God in its immeasurable dimensions grounded in God's wisdom."[6] Nonetheless, the imagery does lend itself in the contemporary discussion to a comprehensive image of the triune life. It includes vertical, horizontal, and expansive dimensions. Thus, the various ways in which the Christian tradition has attempted to articulate the mystery of the Trinity within the confines of human experience can be resumed geometrically into vertical and horizontal lines at the center of which is the death-resurrection of Jesus with all four outer points connected by lines so that the whole represents the force field of the divine life. Visually, the figure is as follows:

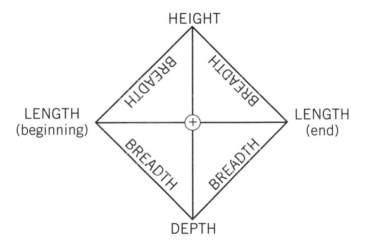

The vertical height and depth represent the *mystical praxis* of seeking to transcend time and space in the ecstatic experience of the eternal embrace of God; the length represents the *emancipatory praxis* of seeking to realize in time and space—from creation to eschaton— the full and final liberation of the children of God in God's kingdom; but it is the breadth that affords a *comprehensive image* of the totality as inclusive of both mystical and emancipatory concerns. The image is of God as one in whom there is room for another. Identity through self-transcendence, reaching beyond oneself to others and withdrawing oneself (one's *ego*) to make room for others, is proposed by Bernd

Jochen Hilberath as a way of inferring from the self-realization of human persons insight into the Holy Spirit as person. "...the self-transcendence of God, as it is revealed in the Father who graciously devotes himself to his creation, and in the Son who abases himself for the salvation of the world, and in the Holy Spirit who makes space for the creation to breathe freely, belongs to God's essence, from which the creation lives and to which it orients itself."[7] His final conclusion embraces the vertical, horizontal, and comprehensive dimensions. "Living out of the Holy Spirit of God means: to accept life as a gift; to give room to other life, to live in relationship, to allow oneself to be liberated and to liberate others, and in all engagements to await the consummation from God."[8] The image of God's *kenōsis*, that is, of God's withdrawal so as to allow the created universe to emerge through the self-actualizing energy inherent within the creation itself, is an important one in contemporary trinitarian thinking. It comes to its focal intensity in Jesus' freely given obedience unto death on the cross and in the Spirit's transformation of Jesus into the glory of the Father through the resurrection. This is the love of Christ that passes beyond all knowledge. The Letter to the Ephesians does not emphasize the suffering of the cross (see 2:16) so much as "the riches of his glory" and "the overwhelming greatness of his power" manifest in the resurrection and exaltation of Christ so that Christ now rules over "every rule and authority and power and lordship" (1:17–21). The fourfold reference indicates in spatial terms completeness and comprehensiveness. What more, then, does "all the fullness of God" refer to?

The third *hina* clause speaks of being filled into (*eis*) all the fullness of God. This forms a kind of inclusion with the Father (v. 14) from whom every family in the heavens and on earth is named. The dynamic sense of movement rather than rest seems also to be the intention of the Gospel of John, who speaks of the Son (*monogenēs theos*) "being always into (*eis*) the bosom of the Father" (1:18). The Son who knows the Father in the deepest and most intimate way possible is the one who has made him known. Similarly, when the Beloved Disciple first appears, he is pictured as resting "in the bosom of Jesus" (13:23). The dynamic here as in Ephesians is a movement of the whole universe (however differently interpreted then as now) toward the Father.[9] The theocentric view of both the Hebrew and Christian Scriptures always identifies "the God" (*ho theos*) as the Father. Yet, in Ephesians that fullness is identified with

4

Christ as the head and with the Church as his body (see Col 1:18–19; 2:9–10). This raises crucial issues for trinitarian thinking that we will examine later. For the moment it is important to note two extremes that should be avoided.[10] One is to lose sight of the absolute transcendence of the triune life and to reduce the Trinity in one way or another to an identification with the processes of creation. The other is to so separate the inner divine life (the immanent Trinity) from the divine involvement in the creative process (the economic Trinity) that there appears to be an unbridgeable chasm between God *in se* and God *pro nobis*, especially in terms of a realistic (as opposed to a merely nominal or conceptual) understanding of God's relationship to the world. The genius of Scripture is that it has maintained in tensive identification the absolute transcendence of God and the complete immanence[11] of God in the world (cosmos). Only the absolutely transcendent can be completely immanent (present) to the whole and to each part in its specific and concrete particularity without being reduced to any one part. The incarnation affirms an identification with a particular human life but without losing the divine transcendence. Similarly, the Church (in the person of the Beloved Disciple in John) and through the Church the whole cosmos is invited to "enter into the total fullness of God" (as Schnackenburg translates 3:19). What that fullness entails is the subject matter of a trinitarian Christology.

This initial focus on Paul's prayer in Ephesians has raised a number of questions: about the nature of God's glory and power and how it is communicated; about the expansive character of the universe and how it is to be interpreted; about the transcendence and immanence of the triune life who is always and only known as a "God for us." We will engage these and other questions in the course of the book but, before proceeding, it will be helpful to clarify the approach of the present study toward an integrated trinitarianism by setting it in contrast to the recent much discussed and controverted proposal of Roger Haight in his book *Jesus Symbol of God*.[12] While the following focuses upon points of difference as a way of clarifying my own approach, it is important to state at the outset in positive terms why this book is important and why it should be widely read and discussed.[13] First, the book provides a tremendously wide range of sources and resources. Haight has clearly read not only widely but well, with a depth of understanding of the field of Christology. He offers balanced and clear summaries of a great variety of views, including many with which he disagrees. Second, the book raises all the crucial questions and sets them out in an orderly and clear fashion. One may disagree with his views but he challenges the reader to reflect more critically on the foundations for their own views. Third, the method of the book, described as a critical hermeneutical method of correlation, rightly calls for fidelity to the tradition while rendering it intelligible, credible, and empowering in our contemporary world. The constant engagement with the postmodern world is very helpful in the execution of such a task.

Nonetheless, there are crucial differences between Haight's approach and my own. My purpose here is not to review the book as a whole but to highlight five key issues that will give context to the present work and render it more intelligible.[14] The five issues are: (1) the understanding of genetic method; (2) the centrality of the resurrection; (3) Jesus as the cause of salvation; (4) Logos and Spirit Christologies as pluralistic alternatives; (5) concern for the human Jesus, especially his human freedom.

1. *Understanding genetic method*: Haight speaks of "a genetic structure of understanding" that begins foundationally "from below" and entails an ascending Christology (40). I have always found the language "from below" and "from above," while it is frequently employed, to be unnecessary and misleading because it sets up an implied opposition between Jesus' humanity and divinity. While I agree that one should begin Christology with an analysis of the historical development from Jesus to the early Church, one should seek the point of synthesis (Haight refers to a "center of gravity") that holds the whole together. Haight finds it in the human, historical Jesus of Nazareth. I find it in the death and resurrection of Jesus. While the emphasis upon the dialectical character of Christology (204–207) is valid, I would answer the questions that follow from it quite differently given the different "center of gravity." This will be evident in the other points that follow.

2. *The centrality of the resurrection*: Haight speaks of "uncentering" the resurrection (149). This is the main point where I differ because everything else flows from this view. Haight maintains that the resurrection is the condition of the possibility of Christology (207–209) but only as a "conceptual symbol." The resurrection releases Jesus from his historical particularity and makes him universally available for a pluralistic variety of christological constructions. For Haight, a "concrete

symbol" is a person, event, or thing; a "conceptual symbol" is a concept, word, or story. Jesus of Nazareth is a concrete symbol but not Jesus as risen. Haight does say that Jesus is truly risen into life with God, but Jesus as truly transformed by the creative power of the Spirit so that he now lives as the fully human one ("Son of Man") in his personal identity gets no consideration. In my view, Jesus as risen, even more than the historical Jesus of Nazareth, is a concrete symbol. Christology has always been about the identity and reality of Jesus as a *person*. The synthetic key that integrates all we say about Jesus is the Father's creative act in raising him from the dead through the power of the Holy Spirit. This has powerful implications for trinitarian Christology, as we shall see.

3. *Jesus as the cause of salvation*: Haight holds a normative but pluralist position so that the normativity of Jesus for Christians can be available for dialogue with other religions while respecting their own claims to normativity. "I propose the thesis that the normativity of Jesus does not exclude a positive appraisal of religious pluralism and that Christians may regard other world religions as true, in the sense that they are mediations of God's salvation" (411). He affirms that the "key step or point of transition to the pluralist position is the breakdown of a causal connection between Jesus of Nazareth, who is the basis of Christology, and the salvation that according to Christian faith goes on outside the Christian sphere" (422). The analysis of the four positions (399–400) into exclusivism, constitutive inclusivism, normative but nonconstitutive, and pluralism fails to consider another alternative: constitutive but nonnormative. In my view, the resurrection is the constitutive cause of salvation for the whole of creation whereas normativity here refers to continuity and coherence within the particular tradition of Christian faith. In other words, the effectiveness of Jesus' resurrection in the power of the Spirit is available to other religious mediations even though they do not recognize the specifically Christian claims about Jesus. In this sense, Jesus as risen in his eternal relation to the Father transcends all religions, including Christianity.[15]

4. *Logos and Spirit Christologies as pluralistic alternatives*: Haight proposes a questioning of and so reinterpretation of Karl Rahner's christological language (432–445). This is perhaps the most important section of the whole book because he seeks to demonstrate the validity of his pluralist thesis by setting up Logos as a simple parallel alternative to

7

Spirit. To do this he returns to the metaphorical/figurative usage of Wisdom, Word, Spirit in the Hebrew Bible as ways of talking about divine immanence while maintaining divine transcendence. As a consequence he denies the radically new claim of John 1:14 that moves not only from preexistence to incarnation but from personification to person. There seems to be no room for the classical understanding of Irenaeus and others that moves from creation to covenant to incarnation, the last being the most radical gift of God's self-communication, that is, the gift of God's very Self in the person of the Son. Moreover, the Christian Scriptures from Paul to John clearly differentiate between Jesus as the Son and the Spirit. The central image is not Logos but Son. Haight's appeal to the pluralism of christologies in the Christian Scriptures (178–184) leads to a rather arbitrary selection of the Synoptics over John that ignores any notion of a development, a deepening insight into the mystery under the guidance of the Holy Spirit (which would assume the integrity of the canon under the inspiration of the Spirit). In his treatment of the "foundational metaphor" (he prefers "empowerment" rather than incarnation; I prefer resurrection), he confuses literal language with empirical demonstration. "The language of incarnation, of God as Logos assuming flesh, is not literal language in which the referent is an object of this wordly knowledge and definition. We do not *know* God as Logos; God is an object of belief, which is an expression of faith-hope....The foundational metaphor of incarnation cannot appear credible when it is reduced to digital, empirical, or literal non-symbolic language" (439, italics in original). While it is true that we cannot demonstrate by the use of empirical methods the reality of the incarnation, it is not true to say that we cannot affirm it literally.[16] Haight cannot accept the language of Ephesus (Cyril of Alexandria's second letter to Nestorius that employs the phrase *henōsis kat' hypostasin* = unity according to hypostasis) that the human Jesus is *really* (that is, literally) constituted in existence by the eternal Word. He prefers the "Antiochene mode" to the Alexandrian, with the result that his reinterpretation of Rahner becomes a modalist position. In my view, neither the Alexandrians nor the Antiochenes adequately articulate the Gospel of John, whose genius was precisely to tell the whole story of Jesus as one who was (and is) inseparably human and divine. As we shall see, the basis for all subsequent christological and hence trinitarian reflection is the story of Jesus as both the source and the goal of all theories and conceptualizations.[17]

5. *Concern for the human Jesus, especially his human freedom*: Haight says that "the Spirit enhances Jesus' freedom rather than acts in its stead" (459). The same could be said of the Logos understood in the classical sense. One of the great advances of contemporary biblical scholarship, to which Haight gives a great deal of attention, is that it has given us a Jesus with a much more human face. In my view, this should not displace the traditional Logos Christology but it should qualify it so that the self-expression of the divine Word incarnationally is the human subjectivity of Jesus.[18] The hypostatic unity does not negate the full exercise of human freedom in Jesus. Rather, it is unity with the divine that brings Jesus to the fullness (*plērōma*: Col 1:19; 2:9) of what it is to be human. In him we see revealed the intention of God for the fullness of human life from the beginning of creation to its consummation proleptically realized in Jesus' death and resurrection.

The approach of the present study, in contrast to Roger Haight's effective dismissal of the immanent Trinity as merely a matter of abstract speculation, seeks to develop an integrated trinitarianism that affirms both Spirit and Word within the divine life and in the economy of salvation. In the light of contemporary emphases on a renewed Spirit Christology, however, it seeks to include a more "robust pneumatology."[19] As David Coffey puts it, "...Spirit Christology provides our best mode of access to the theology of the Trinity."[20] Yet, as he also says, Spirit Christology to be successful must incorporate Logos Christology and vice versa in order to be adequate to the tradition grounded in the scriptural data. We will treat his "return" model later but his view as to how we *know* the immanent Trinity should be mentioned at the outset. "The view that I advocate, in line with the epistemology of Lonergan, is that corresponding to the three stages of knowing in general, apprehension, understanding, and judgment, there are three levels of knowledge of the Trinity, the data of the New Testament, the immanent Trinity, and the economic Trinity."[21] However, he recognizes a difference for the unique case of the Trinity: "...in the Trinity *two* judgments are made, the first being that the immanent Trinity exists of itself not just at the level of abstraction but really and actually, that is, *in itself*, and the second being that it exists also in the return to the New Testament data, that is, as precisely the economic Trinity."[22] According to the schema of Lonergan, the level of understanding remains the level of abstraction so that the affirmation that the Trinity truly exists as understood can only be made at the level of the economic Trinity. In an earlier work, Coffey states: "The proper study of the Trinity is the study of the economic Trinity, which of course presupposes both the biblical and the immanent Trinity." He explains:

> when we consider this triple-layered structure of knowing in relation to our knowledge of the Trinity, we see that the biblical data, what we have called the biblical Trinity, are the "matter to be known", inasmuch as they are the primary data of revelation. The immanent Trinity is our understanding of these data in the world of our own intellectual culture, which has been formed, at least initially, by the ontological categories of Hellenism. Finally, the doctrine of the economic Trinity is our affirmation that *this* is the case. It is the judgment by which we return from our reflective understanding to the real spiritual world brought to its perfection in the Christ event, and this not just as revealed and experienced but as understood and affirmed.[23]

Thus, the only verification for the abstract speculations of the understanding lies in the judgment that there is a correspondence between the data and the conceptualizations of it. This judgment affirms at one and the same time that the economic Trinity is the reality of the immanent Trinity and vice versa. Put another way, the only God we know is the God "for us." We can distinguish God as God and God as Creator but for us God as God remains an abstraction (albeit a useful one to maintain the absolute divine transcendence) that can only be verified in the divine self-involvement in the creative process (the divine immanence). Thus, as with Pannenberg, we cannot describe the concrete reality of God apart from his specific acts in history.[24] Or, as Walter Kasper puts it, rephrasing Rahner's basic axiom, "...in the economic self-communication the intra-trinitarian self-communication is present in the world in a new way, namely, under the veil of historical words, signs and actions, and ultimately in the figure of the man Jesus of Nazareth. The need is to maintain not only the kenotic character of the economic Trinity but also its character of graciousness and freedom in relation to the immanent Trinity and thus to do justice to the immanent mystery of God *in* (*not: behind!*) his self-revelation."[25]

In order to explore the implications of all this for a trinitarian Christology we will first seek to articulate the contemporary context in terms of evolutionary science, language about s/Spirit, and ecumenical overtures (chapter 1). Then we will examine the data of experience in the biblical narratives with special attention to how the whole story of Jesus is rooted in the paschal mystery (chapter 2). This, in turn, gives rise to the efforts to understand the triune God of Christian faith in the patristic conceptualizations that culminate in the most universally accepted ecumenical creed formulated at the first Council of Constantinople in 381 (chapter 3). Finally, we will explore the judgment that the economic Trinity *is* the immanent Trinity as exemplified in three contemporary Western theologians who in various ways open up the possibility of a rapprochement with Eastern trinitarianism. The "social" model of Jürgen Moltmann, the "return" model of David Coffey, and the "interactive" model of Thomas Weinandy offer different perspectives for such a rapprochement. Are they compatible or contradictory? The final conclusion will affirm an integrated trinitarianism as having the ultimately practical effect of revealing and communicating the one and only power that sets us free.[26]

CHAPTER ONE

Context:
An Emergent Universe

1. The Horizons of Evolutionary Science

The most important social location for contemporary theologians is the world of science. Cultural concerns about appropriate theological language, religious concerns about meaningful dialogue with other traditions, social concerns about the emancipation of the poor and the marginalized[1] converge in a universal care and concern for being, not in an abstract sense of being in itself, but in each and every particular being. Science does abstract from the particular insofar as it seeks patterns and regularities (statistical probabilities) but theology, while it must maintain an unceasing openness to the new and unforeseen possibilities that science affords and must integrate them into its vision, cannot but understand the whole in terms of the concrete and particular. Theology is about the intrinsic value, the dignity and integrity, of each particle in the universe because it celebrates a divine reality that is dynamically and personally present to each from the beginning of creation to the end.

Science within certain defined limits can get along perfectly well without theology, but theology needs the experience of the world that only science can give. While concern for the human remains vital, science moves us beyond anthropocentrism, challenges many of our assumptions, and enriches our understanding. Here, the most important question for the theologian is not so much *whether* God acts or interacts with creation but "what is the character of the *creation* in which God acts and with which God interacts?"[2] Science provides new and hitherto unimagined possibilities. "No serious theologian can ignore these new horizons. These are the revelatory thresholds of our time, calling us to encounter ultimacy and meaning in a novel and challenging context. God comes alive in our world, and the divine permeates on a scale our limited imaginations can only vaguely comprehend. Our world is narrating the sacred story with new symbols, new language, and above all with a new cosmology."[3]

The issue of science and religion has produced a plethora of resources. For the sake of simplicity and clarity, I will focus on four questions and on one author as an exemplification of each. First, how far does the logic of scientific rationality take us into "the mind of God" (Paul Davies)? Second, in what sense can the unfolding of cosmic evolution be understood as "God's story" (Diarmuid O'Murchú)? Third, does God have a vision of the future that is differently revealed in the openness of creation to "novelty" (John F. Haught)? Finally, how does Jesus embody the divine intention for the fullness of "the human being" (Walter Wink)? In all of this, we must not forget the need to integrate the shadow side of our human experience. As Neil Ormerod reminds us, theology must always remind the sciences of the problem of evil and the limits of science.[4] Nonetheless, we must retain the utopian hope of future convergence. As C. G. Jung puts it: "Sooner or later, nuclear physics and the psychology of the unconscious will draw closer together, as both of them independently of one another and from opposite directions, push forward into transcendental territory."[5] Can the same be said of theology and science?

The Mind of God. Is a theory of everything (TOE) or a grand unified theory (GUT) possible, as many physicists, including Stephen Hawking, think? "However, if we do discover a complete theory, it should in time be understandable in broad principle by everyone, not just a few scientists. Then we shall all, philosophers, scientists, and just ordinary people, be able to take part in the discussion of the question of why it is that we and the universe exist. If we find the answer to that, it would be the ultimate triumph of human reason—for then we would know the mind of God."[6] Indeed, how is it that we know something rather than nothing, and why is it that we don't know everything? Paul Davies has "come to the point of view that mind—that is, conscious awareness of the world—is not a meaningless and incidental quirk of nature, but an absolutely fundamental facet of reality."[7] In a key chapter, he speaks of "the mathematical secret" and asks why mathematics is at the very heart of science. If our human intellectual powers are determined by biological evolution, as some would say, why is it that they are tuned to the extravagant quest of understanding the entire universe (referring to John Barrow)? The human brain has a dual capacity for knowing the world. One is the kind of direct perception that we share with the animal world and that serves the biological need for survival. The other is the power of abstract reasoning, as the "unreasonable effectiveness of mathematics" (Eugene Wigner), that serves no apparent biological need. Indeed, we can know something without knowing everything because, while the world is an interconnected whole, we must attend to individual parts in the various scientific specializations for progress to be made at all. Science "works" and so inseparably does mathematics.[8] Paul Davies offers a very readable and profound exposition of scientific rationality, but he ends not so much with the mystery of God, although he is open to the possibility of mystical experience, as with the mystery of mind.

> The central theme that I have explored in this book is that, through science, we human beings are able to grasp at least some of nature's secrets. We have cracked part of the cosmic code....The physical species *Homo* may count for nothing, but the existence of mind in some organism on some planet in the universe is surely a fact of fundamental significance. Through conscious beings the universe has generated self-awareness. This can be no trivial detail, no minor byproduct of mindless, purposeless forces. We are truly meant to be here.[9]

If the universe is aware of itself, what is our role as humans if not to bring an appreciation to that awareness? Whether one holds for the strong or the weak anthropic principle,[10] the fact is that we are here to observe it. Our role, in my view, is not to endorse an anthropocentric view as if humans were the center and purpose of the universe, but to contemplate beauty as the *most* "reliable guide to truth."[11] From a faith perspective, after all, our story is really God's story.

The Story of God. Can we imagine a story that is greater than ourselves? That is the question of Diarmuid O'Murchú. He believes, in fact, that we must allow the universe to tell its own story.[12] In doing so, we will rediscover God, not ourselves, at the center of the story. Beyond the emphasis of scientific evolution on observable, measurable, and quantifiable evidence, he affirms the vision of figures like Teilhard de Chardin and Sri Aurobindo: "to comprehend the nature of consciousness as the key element in a spiritual understanding of the evolutionary process."[13] "Spirit-power" is the driving force or energy of the whole cosmos, and consciousness is the wisdom inherent in the process, which is as a whole future-oriented. A key theme in this understanding is "coevolution," that is, that God cocreates the universe through self-organizing processes. The central challenge is "a radical re-visioning of how we understand the divine to be at work in creation."[14] His favored image of the divine is the "Originating and Sustaining Mystery" as prodigiously creative who "outpaces all our constructs" (both of religion and of science) and who "unceasingly lures us to radically new places and new ways of being."[15] Thus, we should neither exclude God a priori, as do many scientists, nor should we introduce God into the process prematurely, as do many religionists, because, in both cases, we miss the challenge to the imagination of participating in the unfolding processes of life that can reveal to us how the divine actually works in our world.[16]

In sum, we must let go of our "anthropocentric will to power" and recognize the power of consciousness as greater than ourselves. "As a planetary, cosmic species, we belong to a reality greater than ourselves. It is our congruence with our planetary identity and our cosmic potential that bestow genuine power upon us, including the wisdom to befriend our human vulnerability."[17] Our role, once again, is one of contemplative awareness, creation conscious of itself at ever unfolding depths, for the true mystic is one who sees reality as it is so that he or she is free to cooperate in its transformation.[18] In this book, as in his previous one, O'Murchú offers a very helpful review of many of the advances in contemporary science, especially the concomitant insight that everything is interrelated and interdependent. But, for our purposes, the key insight is the inseparability of God and the story of the universe. We must not ignore or bypass the story as it is unfolding in contemporary science but embrace it, enter into it, and participate in it with creative imagination. Indeed, as he says, information, awareness, and imagination are key to the contemporary shift in consciousness.

In his final chapter, "Our Next Evolutionary Leap," O'Murchú maintains that we must move beyond current evolutionary theory that reduces biological creatures to "gene machines" (Richard Dawkins) and focus on life "as an open, creative process." This entails a fourfold agenda of (1) "honoring the universal," that is, the creative energy of an alive and mindful universe that deploys information in new and imaginative ways; (2) "befriending the earth," that is, the earth itself as a life-form (the Gaia theory of James Lovelock); (3) "redefining the human," that is, replacing the anthropocentric will to power and control with a playful participation that is "creative, imaginative, cooperative, and spiritually alert"; and (4) to have trust in "the future" as guaranteed by the God who walks with us in the garden of life.[19]

The Future of God. The key word for John Haught is *novelty*. In this he shares much in common with O'Murchú. In *God After Darwin* Haught maintains the compatibility of religious belief and evolutionary biology. He proclaims Darwinism "a great gift to theology." In *Deeper Than Darwin*, however, he seeks to show that it is not neo-Darwinism ("Darwinian concepts updated by genetics") combined with evolutionary psychology (to explain away the human tendency to be religious) that can provide the deepest or even an adequate explanation of life but religion understood as "a consequence of the presence to consciousness of an Absolute Reality."[20] Thus he proposes a theology of evolution that recognizes the limits of science while seeking to address the intractable mystery of evil. He seeks convergence by locating the confusion between science and religion as a "reading problem" that must take into account the historical narrative of the universe.

> The narrative texture of nature still lies largely unacknowledged. However, once we develop the habit of thinking of the cosmos as a story—as geology, biology, and astrophysics now demand that we do—the universe again becomes something to be read, possibly at many levels of depth. We not only now find in nature features analogous to codes, alphabets, grammars, and information. We can also make out the outline of a dramatic adventure. But shall we be able to find a 'meaning' written there also?[21]

The challenge is to move beyond literalism, whether it is that of evolutionary materialism or of biblical fundamentalism, to greater "depth" so that the texts of Scripture and the book of nature can interpret each other. "Only in the depth beneath the texts of nature and holy writ shall we find a way to reconcile science and religion, evolution and the idea of God."[22]

The key issue is how to reconcile divine providence with the main insights of Darwinian evolution, namely, contingency (chance), necessity (law), and deep cosmic time (as irreversible).[23] In opposition to any form of natural theology or design theory that would argue to divine providence from nature, he argues for a theology of nature or evolution based on the image of God revealed in Scripture, and especially in the paschal mystery, as a self-emptying (kenotic) God who promises a future without predetermining its outcome—a God who would have created precisely the world proposed by evolutionary theory. He says,

> My thesis, however, is that cosmic purpose lies deeper than either Darwin or design. Cosmic purpose is more appropriately thought of in terms of nature's *promise* than of the "design" that appears on the surface of this great text. The idea of "design", in any case, is too brittle to represent the richness, subtlety and depth of the life-process and its raw openness to the future. Life is more than "order". Life requires also the continual admittance of disruptive "novelty", and so the idea of "promise" serves more suitably than "design" to indicate life's and the universe's inherent meaning.[24]

The future of God then is the future of the evolving universe, for this is a God who delights in aesthetic diversity, in beauty as "ordered novelty" (Whitehead), and who invites us along with the whole of creation to be cocreators of such beauty. As humans with reflective awareness, our final destiny or role will be to share with our limited conscious awareness in the ultimate cosmic fulfillment of Absolute Reality.[25] This can only be understood and experienced as a "work of love."[26]

The humanness of God. What was God thinking about when in the fullness of time the Word became flesh (John 1:14), when the Son of God came to us and suffered with us in our weaknesses, tested or tempted like us in all things but without sin (Heb 4:15)? Does it matter in our understanding of God that Jesus comes among us as poor, weak, vulnerable, a victim of imperial power? Does it matter in our understanding of ourselves, of what it means to be human and how to become human? Walter Wink explores the mysterious and enigmatic figure of *the* son of *the* man (double article in Greek) as "a catalyst for human transformation."[27] He draws on Carl Jung's psychology of the unconscious (archetypes): "To use Carl Jung's terms, the son of the man may be considered an image of the archetype of wholeness, which mediates between the transcendent Self and the individual ego." The *ego* is "the conscious aspect of the self, subordinate to the self, and related to the self like a part to the whole." The *self* is "the totality of one's being," which includes the totality of selves and the transpersonal "Self," which psychologically is indistinguishable from God.[28]

Wink proposes a convergence between biblical revelation centered on Jesus' use of "the son of the man" and Jung's understanding of archetypal images to indeed push us forward into transcendental territory, that is, to become the whole selves that the Self (God) wants us to be. "This process of humanizing humanity constitutes the anthropic revelation, that is to say, the revelation of what humanity is meant to be."[29] He sees Ezekiel's vision of the throne chariot (Ezek 1:26—2:1) as the immediate inspiration for Jesus' use of the idiom as a personal self-reference.[30] "I argue that the expression 'the son of the man' is an allusion to Ezekiel, and that 'the man' in that phrase is the divine figure on the throne who calls Ezekiel 'son': the 'son' of the Human One seated on the throne. After Jesus' death, that archetype was writ large as the 'second coming' of Jesus."[31] God as the "Human One" becomes incarnate in the person and mission of Jesus as the child of the "Human One" who reveals in creative and new ways the vision of what it means to be fully human.

Wink offers an excellent and comprehensive review of all the references to the Son of Man image, biblical and extrabiblical, pre-Easter and post-Easter sayings of Jesus, and including Jewish mysticism and Gnosticism. Whatever one thinks of his view that "Jesus as the son of the man is enough" for Christianity and that he wants "to worship the God Jesus worshipped, not worship Jesus as God,"[32] his emphasis upon the archetypal image of "the son of the man" as the psychic bearer of God's intention that we become human as God is human affords an important and striking insight into God's relation to us as humans. We are to become what God has fully intended *us* to be. The "christological revelation" of God's desire to become incarnate has as its result the "anthropological revelation" of what God desires us to be.

The future of the "Human Being" is an open future that depends on the creative response of human beings. As a catalytic agent for transformation that lures us forward, the future of the "Human Being" depends on the Holy Spirit as "the active agent that *effects* the change into who we are meant to be."[33] Jesus through his Spirit empowers us to act as the "Human Being."

Wink concludes:

> It is this study's judgment that Jesus did indeed utter a number of the pre-Easter son-of-the-man sayings in the Gospels; that he expressed the core of the suffering sayings, in that he did anticipate his execution; and that he looked forward to the transformation of human beings into the fuller humanity exemplified and made possible by Jesus as the Human Being. That churches developed additional sayings is only to be expected. That they were not always true to his meaning goes without saying. Scholars have erred, however, by applying exclusively rational categories to what are essentially archetypal images. These images were precipitated involuntarily from the unconscious as indications from the psychic depths about the significance of Jesus' life. Their truth lies not in their historicity but in their faithful rendering of the intrapsychic transformations taking place in believers after the ascension, that is, after Jesus entered the archetype of the Human Being. That is the real miracle of Easter.[34]

Thus, for Wink, Jesus is the bearer of an archetypal power greater than himself and he should not be made into the sole bearer of what it means to be human. Rather, he is the "revealer and catalyst of our true humanity"[35] which we are all called to create in new and unforeseen ways.

In conclusion, the horizons of evolutionary science as context for trinitarian Christology must explore the powers of the human mind, the great story of cosmic evolution, human awareness of beauty as "ordered novelty," and the emergence into consciousness of a collective awareness of what it means to be human. All four authors would agree that a truly emergent universe cannot be simply predicted or predetermined. There is a radical openness to the future as God's future.

Christian faith has understood the effective power of that future to be the advent of the Holy Spirit.

2. Advents of the Spirit

The poet Gerard Manley Hopkins compares the Virgin Mary to the air we breathe: "wild air, world mothering air, nestling me everywhere." The image is most applicable to the Holy Spirit as well. The Spirit is so deeply present to our inmost selves (compare St. Augustine's famous dictum: *"Deus interior intimo meo"* in the *Confessions* III, 6, 11) that we are usually unaware of the presence and power of the one who sighs within us (Rom 8:26). It is the same creative Spirit that gently and persuasively draws cosmic order out of chaos, continually renews the face of the earth (Ps 104:30), and draws humankind into the unutterable experience of transcendent beauty. Many today recognize that we have either forgotten or neglected the pervasive centrality and importance of the Holy Spirit not only for our personal lives but most signally for the cosmos as a whole.[36]

The retrieval of the Spirit raises a number of issues that are both new and old (Matt 13:52). Kilian McDonnell insists quite rightly that we must not now replace a Christomonism with a Pneumatomonism. He calls for a *trinitarian* theology of the Holy Spirit that makes up for "the lack of a fully reflective teaching on the Spirit in the Scriptures themselves" by developing a proper role (*proprium*) for the Spirit.[37] Basically, as McDonnell points out, there can be no experience of the Spirit that is not materially an experience of Christ. Christology and pneumatology must always go together. Irenaeus's image of "the two hands of the Father" should mean, according to trinitarian logic, that the mission of the Son and the mission of the Spirit in the order of salvation are equally important, though distinctive or proper to each. McDonnell's principal emphasis is upon the Spirit's "contact function."[38]

> In functional terms (obviously not ontologically) the Spirit is the point of contact between God and humankind. Therefore, when one builds a theology, one does not start with a consideration of God, nor with humankind in itself. One starts at the point where the one "touches" the other. One starts with the historical experience (individual and

collective) of the Spirit, which is the obverse side of the Spirit's mission. The Spirit who is experienced in history is the point of contact between God and humankind, the point where "the perfect Father" through the Son touches history and therefore the Church, but in another direction the Spirit is the point of entry into the mystery of Christ through which the mystery of the Father is attained.[39]

Thus, in the Spirit the Father through the Son "touches" history and we through the Son "enter" into the mystery. While there is a twofold mediation of Word and Spirit, there is a *functional* immediacy proper to the person of the Spirit. The trinitarian control of the Spirit's mission is "from the Father to the Father" expressed more fully in the liturgical pattern: from the Father through the Son in the Spirit to the Father.[40] In theological reflection, Christ is the "what" (content as object) and the Spirit is the "how" (contact as the interpretive perspective that permeates all of theology). "Pneumatology determines the 'rules' for speaking about God."[41]

McDonnell's focus is on the two equal but distinct missions of the Son and the Spirit and hence on the economic Trinity. In sum: "Within the rhythm of the economic Trinity, the Spirit exercises a contact function, giving pneumatology a hermeneutic role."[42] If, as quoted above, one starts theology with the historical experience of the Spirit and the Spirit is "a way of knowing Jesus and the Father," then it is crucial to know what this experience is and where it comes from. Images come to mind that are personal and relational, mother, lover, friend, as well as tactile and affectionate, a "touch," a "kiss," an "embrace."[43] The evocative power of biblical language and mystical experience does need systematic reflection in a hermeneutic that recognizes the power and limits of human language even as a reflection of divine self-communication. We will employ the sequence, advocated by David Coffey, of moving from the biblical data to the abstract conceptualization of the data in terms of the immanent Trinity to the twofold judgment that the immanent Trinity as truly existing in itself is the same Trinity experienced in the economy but present in a new way (Walter Kasper). The immanent Trinity is present in his self-revelation and only so accessible to us. This corresponds to McDonnell's insistence that the starting point for trinitarian theology must be the historical experience of the Spirit.

But, if the Spirit exercises this "contact function" as a way of knowing Jesus and the Father, then we must move beyond the "rich triadic teaching" of the New Testament[44] to the understanding and affirmation of three "persons" as foundational. This was the approach of the Cappadocians Basil the Great, Gregory of Nazianzen, and Gregory of Nyssa, as distinct from the more abstract approach of starting with the essence of God and then arguing to the Trinity by psychological or ontological analogies.[45] This difference gives rise to a number of questions that cannot be answered without a genuine ecumenical dialogue between East and West. How can we or should we define *person* as applicable to the trinitarian life? What is the distinct or proper role of each "person" in the economy, and do these roles correspond to the distinctiveness of each "person" in the immanent Trinity? Is our access to the immanent Trinity best understood through the mediation of "energies" (St. Gregory Palamas) and/or through the ecstatic experience of "doxology" (Jürgen Moltmann)? How essential is the *taxis* (internal ordering) as proposed by Athanasius and the Cappadocians, that is, the Father as the only source (*pege*), the Son as begotten (*gennesia*), and the Spirit as proceeding (*ekporeusis*), especially insofar as it touches the *filioque*? Does the focus on the Father as origin inevitably lead to the Father as the essential deity and to the Son and Spirit as derivative and so subordinate? Is the Spirit unequivocally the "Spirit of Christ" (Rom 8:9) if the Father is the unique source of the inner life of the Trinity and of the missions in the order of salvation?[46] Finally, from what may be a more Western perspective, how does one understand time and eternity, the finite and the infinite, in relation to the internal dynamics of trinitarian life? Is the eschatological consummation of history, as proposed by Moltmann and Pannenberg, internally constitutive of that life?[47] In order to gain an appropriate context for a Western rapprochement, we must first seek to understand the essential approach and insights of Eastern Orthodoxy as grounded in the patristic tradition of St. Ignatius of Antioch to St. John Damascene.

3. Ecumenical Overture: A View from the East

There are two issues that are crucial to the East–West dialogue: the Western interpolation of the *filioque* into the Nicene-Constantinopolitan Creed of 381 and the Eastern rejection and/or radical qualification of

Pope Leo's *Tomus ad Flavianum* as used in the profession of faith at the Council of Chalcedon in 451. Both have been the subject of inter-faith dialogues in recent times.[48] To enter into these dialogues, it is first important to understand the viewpoint of the Eastern Churches. Contemporary theologians such as John Meyendorff, Vladimir Lossky, and John Zizioulas, among others, provide such an opportunity. For Lossky, the dogmatic question of the procession of the Holy Spirit was not

> ...a fortuitous phenomenon in the history of the Church. From the religious point of view, it is the sole issue of importance in the chain of events which terminated in the separation. Conditioned, as it may well have been, by various factors, this dogmatic choice was—for the one party as for the other—a spiritual commitment, a conscious taking of sides in a matter of faith.

And further: "The *filioque* was the primordial cause, the only dogmatic cause, of the breach between East and West. The other doctrinal disputes were but its consequences."[49]

The "mystical theology of the Eastern Church" is a spirituality grounded in the Orthodox dogmatic tradition understood primarily not in terms of conceptual clarification but in terms of a living faith that reveals the divine mystery with the supremely practical goal of attaining union with God through deification (*theōsis*). Fundamental is the recognition that all true theology is apophatic, exemplified by Moses drawing near to God in the darkness of Sinai. The divine nature or essence is absolutely transcendent and incomprehensible. Hence, the function of kataphatic or affirmative theology is to employ images of God's manifestations ("energies") as revealed in scripture, dogmas, liturgies, and ecstatic experiences in order to move toward communion with the living God. The apophatic principle, however, prevents theology from being reduced to philosophical speculation about concepts that would displace the spiritual reality of the mystery.

> The apophatic attitude gave to the Fathers of the Church that freedom and liberality with which they employed philosophical terms without running the risk of being mis-

understood or of falling into a "theology of concepts". Whenever theology is transformed into a religious philosophy (as in the case of Origen) it is always the result of forsaking the apophaticism which is truly characteristic of the Eastern Church.[50]

The revelation of the Trinity is the primordial fact, the given, that cannot be deduced from any system of philosophy. The three persons constitute the very nature or essence of God so that one must maintain a balance between the one nature and the three persons and not stress one at the expense of the other, as appears to be the Western tendency in the *filioque*. While the principle of unity is the person of the Father, this is not a logical priority but the ontological constitution of the very essence of God as differentiated according to the manner proper to each hypostasis. "Understood apophatically, the relation of origin describes the difference but nevertheless does not indicate the manner of the divine processions. 'The mode of generation and the mode of procession are incomprehensible,' says St. John Damascene."[51]

St. Gregory Palamas gave doctrinal precision to the common patristic view that the divine, uncreated "energies" make God who is inaccessible in his essence accessible to his creatures. The energies

> are not effects of the divine cause, as creatures are; they are not created, formed *ex nihilo*, but flow eternally from the one essence of the Trinity. They are the outpourings of the divine nature which cannot set bounds to itself, for God is more than essence. The energies might be described as that mode of existence of the Trinity which is outside of its inaccessible essence.[52]

There is only one essence or nature of God but God exists both in the divine essence and outside it by communicating the uncreated energy of divine grace that enables human beings, while remaining creatures, to become divinized. The Western distinction between uncreated and created grace is not a consideration. The Holy Spirit communicates the divine energy of grace to us so that we may live the very life of Father, Son, and Spirit who dwell within us in the personal manner appropriate to each.

Thus the theology of the Eastern Church distinguishes in God the three hypostases, the nature or essence, and the energies. The Son and the Holy Spirit are, so to say, personal processions, the energies natural processions: The energies are inseparable from the nature, and the nature is inseparable from the three Persons. These distinctions are of great importance for the Eastern Church's conception of mystical life.[53]

If we participate in the divine life through grace, it is important to realize that creation itself is a grace. There is no state of "pure nature." In contrast to Greek philosophy with its notion of the cosmos as a necessary return to the circle of perfection, the crucial difference in Christianity is the affirmation that creation *ex nihilo* (2 Macc 7:28; Rom 4:17) is a free act of God known by revelation, an act proper to a God who is personal and whose common will, belonging to the divine nature, operates according to "volitional thought" (*thelētikē ennoia*, according to St. John Damascene). The created universe is not a platonic replica of the divine essence but something entirely new, fresh from the hands of God. "We might say that by creation *ex nihilo* God 'makes room' for something which is wholly outside of Himself; that, indeed, He sets up the 'outside' or nothingness alongside of His plenitude. The result is a subject which is entirely 'other', infinitely removed from Him, 'not by place but by nature' (*ou topō, alla physei*), as it is expressed by St. John Damascene."[54] The initial state of the created cosmos is an unstable perfection in which created beings must grow in love toward fullness of union with the divine. For humans this presupposes "cooperation," an agreement of wills both divine and human. "The world was created from nothing by the sole will of God—this is its origin. It was created in order to participate in the fullness of the divine life—this is its vocation. It is called to make this union a reality in liberty, in the free harmony of the created will with the will of God—this is the mystery of the Church inherent in creation."[55]

Humans were created in the image and likeness of God (Gen 1:26–27). Humans as persons with intellect and will never cease to be the image of God but will only realize perfect likeness (or assimilation) when fully one with the will of God. True freedom is not a matter of choice (a sign of imperfection) but of the concurrence of the divine will in the uncreated grace given through the Holy Spirit and the human will which submits to God in receiving grace and allowing it to penetrate and transform nature (the individualistic egoism of nature after the original sin) so that the likeness is restored. This is not restoration to an original state of perfection but an eschatological fulfillment of the movement toward union with God, that is, deification.

It is in this context that one understands the twofold economy, or mission, of the Son and the Spirit. The primary concern of the Eastern Churches is with salvation as the supreme goal of creation. This includes the divinization of humanity in the hypostatic unity of the Son and the divinization of the many in the pentecostal outpouring of the Spirit that constitutes the "one, holy, catholic, and apostolic" communion of the Church.

With regard to the work of the Son, Aloys Grillmeier on the basis of the *Codex Encyclius*, a collection of documents on Chalcedon dating to 457–459, indicates that the bishops related Chalcedon to the *kerygma* and the *symbolum* of baptismal catechesis rather than to the subtle distinctions between *hypostasis* and *physis*. The struggle over concepts emerged later, especially when Timothy Aelurus of Alexandria was combating the radical Eutychians.[56] The so-called neo-Chalcedonians were able to accept Chalcedon as a condemnation of Eutyches' denial that Christ is consubstantial to us in his humanity but insisted on the formula of Cyril of Alexandria (unwittingly taken from Appollinaris of Laodicea): *mia physis tou theou logou sesarkōmenē* = one nature of God the Word enfleshed. The non-Chalcedonians rejected Chalcedon on the basis of Leo's language from the *Tomus ad Flavianum* that emphasizes the characteristics proper to each nature, which to them sounded like the Nestorian dualism of two persons. For our purposes, the important point to emphasize is that the Eastern tradition has always maintained with Cyril of Alexandria and the Council of Ephesus (431) the hypostatic unity of the Logos with the flesh, that is, with humanity as such, so that the whole of humanity has been fully realized or consummated in him. "The humanity of Christ is a deified nature that is permeated by the divine energies from the moment of the Incarnation."[57] The human will in Christ is freely subject to the divine will not by freedom of choice (an imperfection) but by freedom of union. The key to understanding the humanity of Jesus is the epiphany at his baptism and his transfiguration, both of which with the resurrection and ascension manifest the glory of the only Son (John 1:14).

According to St. Gregory Palamas, one can distinguish a threefold union: the union according to essence or nature proper to the three Persons in the Trinity and inaccessible to creatures; the union according to *hypostasis* realized in Christ so that in his human nature the divine energies from the Logos penetrate created nature and deify it; the union according to the energy (grace) that is accessible to all those baptized in Christ. "For Palamas, the union 'according to the energy' (or 'by grace') is a union with God himself. This union *with God* is what he seeks to preserve when he insists that the partakable divine energies are *uncreated*. For God is not limited by the concept of essence, transcendent and absolutely inaccessible: he acts, reveals himself, and communicates himself; and man, as the patristic tradition unanimously asserts, was created in the beginning in order to participate in God, without, however, becoming 'God by essence'."[58] God in his essence remains transcendent and free but Jesus' humanity hypostatized by the Logos is the place where human participation in the divine life is forever realized. Our participation is a gift of grace and our response one of thanksgiving (especially in the Eucharist) and of "collaboration" (synergy), but not one of "possession" or "merit."[59]

Hence, if the work of Christ is consummated in his incarnation (uniting the natures and so restoring the true image of God), in his death on the cross (overcoming the power of sin), and in his glorious resurrection (overcoming the final enemy, death), the work of the Holy Spirit is still awaiting its final accomplishment. The key event is Pentecost, which constitutes the Church, for however much the Spirit was operative before or outside the Church, there is a radically new reality here. Pentecost is not the continuation of the incarnation but its sequel or result, the final goal of the divine economy.[60] Yet, the Spirit is always the Spirit of the Son and reveals the Son (1 Cor 12:3) just as the Son reveals the Father (John 1:18).

While the eternal procession of the Spirit is the work of the divine nature, the very *ousia* of God, and so remains unknown and inaccessible to creatures, the temporal mission is the work of the will common to the triune life. The Church as the work of both Christ and the Holy Spirit is an *image* of the Holy Trinity that contains everything necessary to attain the final goal, union with God in perfect *likeness*.

"The work of Christ concerns human nature which He recapitulates in His hypostasis. The work of the Holy Spirit, on the other hand, concerns persons, being applied to each one singly. Within the Church the Holy Spirit imparts to human hypostases the fullness of deity after a manner which is unique, 'personal', appropriate to every man as a person created in the image of God."[61] So Christ unifies and the Spirit diversifies. The goal is the unity of nature realized in a diversity of persons who cease to be individuals. "In truth, we are not here concerned with *individuals* and with *collectivity* but with human *persons* who can only attain to perfection within the unity of *nature*. The Incarnation is the foundation of this unity of nature, Pentecost is the affirmation of the multiplicity of persons within the Church."[62]

In contrast to the West (Augustine and Aquinas), the East does not understand the Holy Spirit as the bond of love between the Father and the Son. "This follows from the fact that the doctrinal tradition of the Eastern Church sees the Father as the sole hypostatic source of the Holy Spirit; the word 'love' (*agapē*), when it is used of the Holy Spirit by the Eastern mystics, does not describe His 'hypostatic character', His position in the Trinity, but always His nature as the giver of love, as the source of love within us, as He who enables us to participate in that supreme perfection of the common nature of the Holy Trinity. For love is 'the very life of the divine nature', in the words of St. Gregory of Nyssa." Nor is this love (grace) understood as a created effect but rather as "an uncreated gift, a divine and deifying energy in which we really participate in the nature of the Holy Trinity, by becoming partakers of the divine nature."[63] If the experience of Christ in the West focuses upon the "imitation of Christ" especially at Gethsemane, the experience in the East focuses upon a new "life in Christ" especially at the Transfiguration. The historical life of Jesus is seen primarily as an epiphany or manifestation of God's glory at his baptism and transfiguration. Hence the contrast: "No saint of the Eastern Church has ever borne the stigmata, those outward marks which have made certain great Western saints and mystics as it were living patterns of the suffering Christ. But, by contrast, Eastern saints have very frequently been transfigured by the inward light of uncreated grace, and have appeared resplendent, like Christ on the mount of Transfiguration."[64]

I have focused in this section on Vladimir Lossky's *The Mystical Theology of the Eastern Church* because it offers a clear and readable presentation of that theology in fundamental agreement with other contemporary theologians of the East and because it includes abundant citations from the patristic sources. In his conclusion, he combines the apophatic with spiritual awareness (*gnōsis pneumatikē*). It is the Spirit who gives us true knowledge and awareness of the triune mystery:

> So, finally, the apophaticism which characterizes the mystical theology of the Eastern Church appears as a witness to the fullness of the Holy Spirit—to this Person who, though He fills all things and brings all things to their ultimate fulfillment, yet remains Himself unknown. In the Holy Spirit all becomes fullness: the world which was created that it might be deified, human persons called to union with God, the Church wherein this union is accomplished; finally, God makes Himself known in the fullness of His Being— the Holy Trinity.[65]

The questions proposed at the end of the second part of this chapter still need to be addressed as we move toward a Western rapprochement with the East. But it was necessary first to offer a summary, albeit far too brief, of at least one very important theological viewpoint of the East. To conclude, is a rapprochement possible? Lossky is more negative. The tradition coming primarily from the biblical and patristic periods

> ...remains common to the East and to the West as far as the Church witnesses with power to those truths which are connected with the Incarnation. But those dogmas which are, so to speak, more inward, more mysterious, those which relate to Pentecost, the doctrines about the Holy Spirit, about grace, about the Church, are no longer common to the Church of Rome and to the Eastern Churches. Two separate traditions are opposed one to another. Even those things which down to a particular moment were held in common receive in retrospect a different stress, appear in a different light as spiritual realities belonging to two distinct experiences.[66]

On the other hand, John Meyendorff in his conclusion sees a convergence between Eastern Orthodoxy's insistence upon the "openness" of the hypostasis (Person of God) to the creature and Karl Rahner's transcendental anthropology of the "openness" of the creature to God. The real distinction between essence and hypostasis allows one to maintain the immutability of the divine essence and at the same time the real change in the hypostatic unity when the Son of God "became flesh." This challenges the understanding that the Persons in the divine essence are *constituted* by internal relations. Rather, the persons in communion are the primordial given in the trinitarian life. "A sound Christology implies, for Rahner, the return to a pre-Augustinian concept of God, where the three hypostases were seen first of all in their personal, irreducible functions, as Father-God, Son-Logos, and the Spirit of God, and not only as expressions of the unique immutable essence."[67] The distinction between the transcendent essence, the hypostatic existence, and the missions in the economy has its roots in the patristic tradition and enables theologians to maintain both the apophatic character of God (absolute transcendence) and God's personal self-involvement in creation (complete immanence that includes a real change of God in the otherness of Jesus' humanity). Meyendorff sees Rahner's view as a return to the "authentic roots" of the patristic tradition that, corresponding to "Christ in Eastern Christian thought" as analyzed in his book, shows an "astonishing relevance" for Western Christian thought in the contemporary world. He concludes: "The ecumenical significance of this discovery is incalculable."[68] We will pursue this in chapter 3 when we consider the ecumenical significance of the Creed of Constantinople and the later addition of the *filioque*.

CHAPTER TWO

Spirit Christology Rooted in the Paschal Mystery

"Spirit Christology provides our best mode of access to the theology of the Trinity," says David Coffey. The Holy Spirit is the point of "contact" between ourselves and the trinitarian life, says Kilian McDonnell. And, in reference to the twofold mission, Bernard Lonergan comments: "Without the visible mission of the Word, the gift of the Spirit is a being-in-love without a proper object; it remains simply an orientation to mystery that awaits its interpretation. Without the invisible mission of the Spirit, the Word enters into his own, but his own receive him not."[1] Thus, the Word incarnate gives content to a love that is made effective by the Spirit. All of this is rooted in the paschal mystery.[2] Hence, this chapter affirms the biblical data as the experiential ground of everything we say about the Trinity, but in the spirit of Philip Rosato's seminal essay, it will advocate "a paschally oriented Spirit Christology" as the fulcrum around which everything revolves in trinitarian thinking.[3] "...a theology of the Trinity might view the paschal event as the glowing point at which the cone-like love-intention of the Father, Son, and Spirit towards the cosmos zeroes in on a momentary point of time and then opens up, again in cone-like fashion, to include the whole of humanity in the dynamic love-energy of the triune God."[4]

The activity of the Spirit is imaged as "a spiraling cone of energy" who at the center point of the paschal mystery reveals the absolute uniqueness of Jesus from the very beginning of his human existence and the universal and cosmic significance of Jesus for the eschatological consummation of the whole of creation. The question, of course, is exactly how this activity of the Spirit is to be understood in relation to the Father and the Son. It is clear that for St. Paul it is the Father (*ho theos*) who raised Jesus from the dead (see, for example, Rom 4:23–25; 6:4; 8:11; 1 Cor

15:15, 38, 57; 2 Cor 4:14–15; Gal 1:1; Phil 2:9–11; 1 Thess 1:10). How then do we understand the Spirit's role in the paschal mystery? Clearly the Spirit is inseparable from the activity of the Father and of the Son. The Father begets and sends but always in the Spirit. The Son is begotten and is the living embodiment of the Father's will in his mission but always in the Spirit. The Spirit is absolutely one yet diversified as the Spirit of the Father and as the Spirit of the Son. Each possesses the Spirit differently and gives the Spirit differently. Thus, true unity differentiates and absolute unity differentiates absolutely. As F. X. Durrwell puts it: the Spirit is "*at the* beginning, in the Father who begets; he is *at the* end in the One Begotten. While proceeding from them, he does not come after the Father or after the Son, for it is in him that they are Father and Son...he is the Person who establishes persons."[5]

The experiential basis for such statements is the human life, death, and resurrection of the Son who is inseparable from the Spirit. "From his birth on earth until the climax at Easter, the sonship of Jesus is displayed in the Holy Spirit; he is truly Son, since he is in truth the man of the Spirit. If then it is possible to ascend from a knowledge of Christ to that of the mystery of the Trinity—than which there is no other, or more sure way—we must conclude that the Father begets in the Spirit, that *he* is the Spirit of the Father in this begetting, that he 'proceeds' in this relationship of Father and Son."[6] Thus, once again, Christology and pneumatology must be thought together. At this point, I will present my view of the development of Christology as evidenced in the Christian Scriptures. The unfolding of Christology centers on the paschal mystery and moves from eschatology to protology, that is, from the end back to the beginning so that the end interprets the beginning and the beginning in turn interprets the end. But my intention is to show that at every point along the way the Spirit is the indispensable agent of this development.

1. The Paschal Mystery

In the parable of the "man who had two sons" (Luke 15:11–32), there is at the crucial turning point the moving and powerful image of the father who, seeing his younger son coming, was "filled with compassion" and ran to him, threw his arms around him, and covered him with kisses (v. 20). Understood allegorically,[7] this is a wonderful and evocative image of the paschal mystery. The Son, though innocent in this case, returns to the Father covered with sin and disfigured by its cruel impact. The Father does not simply receive the Son but embraces him with the power of compassionate love.[8] That is to say, the Father not only identifies with the suffering of the Son but through the creative power of the Spirit transforms death into life (1 Cor 15:54–57). While the image of the Father raising the Son is clear, the important question for a *trinitarian* Christology is the role of the Holy Spirit. To put it crudely, can the Father raise the Son without the active involvement of the Spirit? Paul practically defines the Father as the one who raises Jesus. John frequently indicates a more active role for Jesus himself. Jesus raises himself by his own power (John 2:19; 6:62; 10:17–18; but cf. the three passion predictions in the passive voice at 3:14; 8:28; 12:32) and has the power to raise others (John 5:21, 25–29; 6:39–40, 44, 54; 11:25–26). Yet, neither Paul nor John thinks of the Father or Jesus apart from or independently of the Spirit.

Perhaps the most intriguing biblical text occurs at 1 Corinthians 15:35–57, where Paul turns to the question as posed by the Corinthians: "How are the dead raised? With what kind of body do they come?" (v. 35). James D. G. Dunn proposes that Paul himself probably made the distinction between flesh (*sarx*) and body (*sōma*). "The *flesh* would not be resurrected, but the *body* would. This distinction between flesh and body was a bold and venturesome stroke, for in the general image of the time *sōma* (body) and *sarx* (flesh) were more or less synonymous—both referring to the physical body."[9] While the focus of Paul's theology is upon the eschatological event of Jesus' death and resurrection, his interpretive principle, which takes the form of a commentary on Genesis 1—11 (one could read Romans 1—8 this way), is frequently the fulfillment of God's creative intention. Thus, eschatology always implies protology. This certainly seems to be the case here. Paul begins in vv. 36–41 with the analogy of a seed to indicate continuity that embraces a dialectic of identity and difference based upon the creativity of God: "But God gives it a body as he has chosen, and to each kind of seed its own body" (v. 38).[10] When he applies this to "the resurrection of the dead" in vv. 42–49, however, he employs the contrast language of the Corinthians' dualistic (gnostic and/or apocalyptic) understanding: perishable-imperishable, dishonor-glory, weakness-power, and most significantly *sōma psychikon–sōma pneumatikon*. This is the language of the Corinthians, especially *pneumatikoi* (spiritual ones), *psychikoi* (soul-like ones), and *sarkikoi/sarkinoi* (enfleshed ones), which he uses ironically at 2:6—3:4 to indicate that only one who has the Spirit of God can know the things of God (especially at 2:10–12).

The contrasting pairs culminate in the difference between the first man, Adam (he cites Gen 2:7 at v. 45), whose image we have borne (Gen 1:26–27), and the second man, Christ (cf. vv. 21–22), whose image we will (or should?) bear (v. 49). But the key verse comes at v. 44a. In the context of God's creativity, the verse could be paraphrased to read: It is sown as the Adamic existence under the powers of sin, law, and death (v. 56; cf. Rom 5—7), it is raised as a transformed human existence by the power of God's Spirit (Rom 8:11). The repetition of the word *sōma* understood in the Hebraic sense of the whole person as embodied connotes continuity in the sense that it is the same person but as transformed. The agent of that transformation is the Holy Spirit. Paul is talking here about our resurrection but the logic of his argument here and elsewhere is that we will be raised *as* he was raised. Note his frequent use of *kai* (translated as "likewise," "also," "in the same way") at, for example, Romans 6:5, 8–11; and 8:11 which could be paraphrased: The Father who raised Jesus from the dead will *also* make your dead bodies alive *through* (*dia*) his Spirit dwelling in you. If Jesus raised from the dead is "the first fruits (*aparchē*) of those who have died" (1 Cor 15:20, 23), the seemingly natural conclusion is that our resurrection will be like his (Rom 8:23: "the first fruits of the Spirit") or, perhaps better, we shall participate in our own way in his personal transformation in the Spirit.

This inference is not intended to deny the uniqueness of Jesus as the one who in his own person constitutes the final and definitive act of God's creativity for the salvation of the world, but it is intended to affirm that he himself was constituted as such through the agency of the Spirit and that we participate in that transformation through the agency of the same Spirit. The latter is clear in Paul; the former is an inference from Paul's way of speaking[11] but it does affirm that the Father's activity is always inseparably the action of the Holy Spirit. The Father works through the Holy Spirit and, if this is true in our case, it must be even more true in the case of Jesus' own resurrection. If we are a new creation in Christ (Gal 6:15; 2 Cor 5:17), then the risen Christ is himself a new creation in the sense that he has become completely and fully the "Human One" transformed by the same creative power of the Spirit that accompanied the Word at the beginning of creation (Gen 1:1–3) and animated the first human being as the Lord God's own "breath of life" (Gen 2:7). The creativity of God (the Father) is always accompanied and vivified by the Spirit.

However one may construe the subsequent development of Christology in the early Church, and one might differ on the sequence that I am proposing, the *theological* (= act of God) justification for Christology is the *person* of Jesus who, in this view, has come to the fullness of who he is because at the moment of his death the Father embraced him with the creative, transforming, vivifying power of the Spirit so that now he *is* fully what he always was, the Son. According to Paul's analysis of the human condition under the powers of sin, law (the weakness of humankind's tendency toward sin, the human condition as "flesh"), and death, the risen Christ now lives completely in union with the divine, integrated in his human existence, and beyond the reach of death which he has conquered (Rom 6:9–10; see the whole of Rom 5—8). In traditional language, these three dimensions of human life (lost by Adam's sin and restored by Christ in his death and resurrection) have been referred to as sanctifying grace, integrity, and immortality. Paul does not use this theological language in precisely this way as a reference to the risen Christ, but he does affirm the community's experience of the Spirit who gives life as an experience of the risen Christ: "the last Adam became a life-giving spirit" (1 Cor 15:45b).[12]

2. The Return of Jesus as the Messianic "Son of Man"

The language of resurrection is apocalyptic language intended to signal God's vindication of the just in the face of persecution (Isa 26:7—27:1, especially vv. 14, 19; Ezek 37:11–14; Dan 12:1–3; Wis 2:23ff; 2 Macc 7; 1 Enoch 51; 92:3). Although a return to this life is sometimes envisioned, the apocalyptic hope is to conquer the power of death experienced at the hands of the unjust. It involves a transition from this age to the age to come, that is, to the fulfillment of God's creative intention from the beginning. As such it heralds a new existence beyond death. As an apocalyptic event it can only be known through a revelation from God as Paul indicates in Galatians 1 and 1 Corinthians 15:3–8. Jesus' disciples knew him as one who proclaimed the coming kingdom of God and who, anointed by the Holy Spirit, "went about doing good" (Acts 10:37–38). It is clear that Jesus experienced rejection and persecution, yet maintained the confidence that God would vindicate his mission, a vindication that included not only himself but his disciples who shared in the mission. This may well have been the impact of his use of the image of "the Son of Man" derived from Daniel 7:13, a corporate symbol of divine vindication. A likely expression from Jesus himself would be "the day of the Son of Man" (Luke 17:24, 30).[13] If one combines this apocalyptic image of divine vindication with the apocalyptic event of resurrection as the vindication of *Jesus*, that is, as the personal transformation of Jesus in the power of the Spirit as analyzed above, then "the most primitive Christology of all" would be the identification of Jesus with the Son of Man who was to come.[14] This is a move from a Christology implicit in Jesus' words, deeds, and fate to an explicit Christology: Jesus *is* the Son of Man. Such an affirmation is only possible under the inspiration of the Holy Spirit. As Paul says: "No one can say 'Jesus is Lord' except by the Holy Spirit" (1 Cor 12:3). This would be true of the entire development of explicit Christology.

"Jesus you seek, the Nazarene, the crucified; he has been raised (*ēgerthē*); he is not here" (Mk 16:6; my trans.). Following the Greek word order of this kerygmatic statement helps to bring out the emphasis on the concrete particularity of Jesus. It is *this man Jesus* from the obscure village of Nazareth whom the imperial powers sought to destroy by the humiliating and cruel death of crucifixion that God raised from the dead. Luke in his story of the two disciples on the way to Emmaus (Luke 24:13–35) makes this even more concrete and memorable. It is the *same Jesus* whom we knew prior to his death, the one who walked with us on the way, who explained the Scriptures to us, who came into our homes and broke bread with us—it is the same Jesus but *now transformed* so that he is experienced in the revelatory power of the Spirit. As Paul puts it, what is sown in dishonor and weakness is raised in glory and power. However varied the messianic hopes in Jesus' day, there was certainly no expectation of a crucified Messiah. Rather, the popular hope was for a glorious, reigning Messiah who would destroy the enemies of Israel and establish Israel as the kingdom of God on earth.[15] The great apologetic task of Mark's Gospel was to show that the crucified one is truly the Christ and Son of God who as Son of Man will come again "with great power and glory" (Mark 13:26) and who will judge his accusers (Mark 14:62). The initial expectation of these eschatological events was that he would return soon, and Paul even in his later writings never gave up on the freshness and urgency of that hope.[16] Moreover, it is the Spirit of the risen Christ who guarantees that future (2 Cor 1:21–22; 5:5). The two letters of Paul most concerned about the future *parousia* are contextualized by the power and inspiration of the Holy Spirit (1 Thess 1:5–6; 5:19; 2 Thess 2:8, 13–14). The Spirit who guarantees the future coming of Christ is at the same time the one who enables believers to persevere in the process of transformation (or sanctification) until salvation (the arrival of the kingdom as at 1 Cor 15:20–28) is complete. This is the great theme of Romans 8:11, 14, 16–17, 18–25, 26–27. Nothing in all creation can separate us from the love of God in Jesus who is our Christ and Lord (Rom 8:39). We know this in confident hope "because God's love has been poured into our hearts through the Holy Spirit that has been given to us" (Rom 5:5; cf. 1 Cor 13).

3. The Presence and Power of the Spirit

However much the eschatological expectation of the coming (*parousia*) of Christ remained vivid and fresh—as throughout Paul's writings, in Luke's presentation of the ascension (Acts 1:9–11), in the apocalyptic discourses of the Gospels (Mark 13 par), as well as even to contemporary times—what sustained Jesus' first followers was surely the gift of the Holy Spirit. Hence, Jesus is identified not only as the messianic Son of Man who will return but as the Lord and Christ who "has poured out this that you both see and hear" (Acts 2:33–36). Whether we can actually discern a clearly distinct christological sequence from the expectation of Jesus' return to his exaltation and identification as Lord (*kyrios*), we must recognize that the inclusion of Jesus along with God in cultic devotion was surprisingly early and widespread.[17] Larry W. Hurtado, in contrast to previous attempts to locate the shift to cultic devotion to Jesus in *later* strata of tradition, that is, in a Greek-speaking (Hellenistic) setting, either Gentile or Jewish, argues persuasively that "Christ-devotion" or devotion to Jesus in the "binitarian" sense of reverence for Jesus, an innovation because included within the "exclusivist monotheism" of Israel, was already present in faith and practice among the earliest followers of Jesus in Judea/Jerusalem.[18] Assuming his discussion and agreeing with the "binitarian" character of this devotion, "that Jesus Christ is Lord, to the glory of God the Father" (Phil 2:11), I will focus more on the role of the Holy Spirit in this process as implying a "trinitarian" experience of God. To this end I will consider in turn the experiential basis in Paul, the distinct Pentecostal event in Acts, and the promise of another Paraclete in John.

Paul's letters are suffused with his own religious experience,[19] and he writes out of the creative force of that experience. His intense persecution of the early believers in Jesus is most likely based on their inclusion of Jesus in their devotion to the one God of Israel.[20] Acts 7:55—8:4 makes this association in connection with Stephen's vision of Jesus in the glory of God and Saul's intense persecution, as well as the three accounts of Paul's conversion (Acts 9:1–30; 22:1–21; 26:1–23) with the central focus on *Jesus* whom Saul was persecuting. But it is Paul's own witness that is most telling. His experience was a personal, interior experience of *Jesus* as God's Son whose unique relation to God meant the salvation of all, Jew and Gentile alike, as sons and daughters of God who in the Spirit of his Son can cry *Abba!* (Gal 3.26–28; 4:4–7; Rom 8:14–17). Paul rarely uses the title "Son" but three texts especially evoke the intensity of his personal experience.[21]

"But when God, who had set me apart before I was born and called me through his grace, was pleased to reveal his Son to me [or, in me: *en emoi*], so that I might proclaim him among the Gentiles, I did not confer with any human being, nor did I go up to Jerusalem to those who were already apostles before me, but I went away at once into Arabia, and afterwards I returned to Damascus" (Gal 1:15–17). Three things should be noted. First, Paul understands his experience as a divine election of himself personally and as a revelation whose only source is God, that is, without human mediation. Second, he invokes the phrase "his [God's] son" without any need for explanation because it was the foundational and so common experience of the early followers of Jesus, both Jewish and Gentile. Third, what is new therefore is not the revelation of the Son, which all shared, but the mission to the Gentiles (Gal 2:1–10).

In the second text Paul makes a profoundly personal statement. "But I live, no longer I, rather Christ lives in me [*en emoi*]. But what I now live in the flesh, I live in the fidelity [*en pistei*] of the Son of God, the one who loved me and gave himself over for me" (Gal 2:20; my trans.). One can also translate the genitive as objective, "faith *in* the Son of God," but the foundational virtue of the covenantal relationship is fidelity or loyalty, both God's loyalty to the people and the people's loyalty to God.[22] It was Jesus' own fidelity to the Father's will that brought him to the cross and the Father's fidelity to his Son that raised him from the dead. Paul's experience was surely an intense experience of the faithfulness of Jesus "who gave himself for our sins to set us free…" (Gal 1:4) and of the faithfulness of God the Father "who raised him from the dead" (Gal 1:1; cf. Phil 3:7–11). What appears in the Law as a curse has become the blessing of God. The true fulfillment of the covenantal relationship is the blessing of Abraham understood as "the promise of the Spirit through faith" (Gal 3:13–14).

The third text, which is another very personal statement, this time addressed to the Corinthians, makes the connection with the Spirit even more explicit:

> As surely as God is faithful, our word to you has not been "Yes and No". For the Son of God, Jesus Christ, whom we proclaimed among you, Silvanus and Timothy and I, was not "Yes and No"; but in him it is always "Yes". For in him every one of God's promises is a "Yes". For this reason it is through him that we say the "Amen", to the glory of God. But it is God who establishes us with you in Christ and has anointed us, by putting his seal on us and giving us his Spirit in our hearts as a first installment (2 Cor 1:18–22).

God's fidelity revealed in the fulfillment of God's promises through the "Yes" of the Son enables the community in liturgical settings (cf. 1 Cor 14:16) to say *Amen* to the glory of God. All of this is possible, says Paul, because we have been anointed, sealed, by the gift of the Spirit "in our hearts," the guarantee of our future (2 Cor 5:5). Paul's continuing appeals to the Spirit in 2 Corinthians 3—5 indicates the inseparable connection of the Spirit to his "binitarian" experience of the Son and the Father. Yet, in terms of cultic devotion, the image of Jesus is more usually that of "Lord."[23] Equally, in this use of the title, it is the Spirit that writes "on tablets of human hearts" (3:3); it is the Spirit that "gives life" (3:6); it is the Spirit that removes the veil so that we can have true freedom and can see the glory of the Lord (3:16–18).

This complex passage, in which "Lord" can variously be attributed to the God of Israel (3:16, citing Exod 34:34), to Christ as the image of God (4:4–6), and to the Spirit (3:17–18), indicates the unitive character of the experience as triune. It is the concretely lived experience of being transformed from glory to glory through the power of the Spirit (3:18) and the power of the risen Lord (Phil 3:20–21). It is an experience of God's creative light shining in our hearts. "For it is the God who said, 'Let light shine out of darkness', who has shone in our hearts to give the light of the knowledge of the glory of God in the face of Jesus Christ" (4:6). For Paul this experience is inseparably an experience of the Lord who is the Spirit (3:18). The interior depth of Paul's own experience is well caught at the beginning of his first letter to the Corinthians: "...these things God has revealed to us through the Spirit; for the Spirit searches everything, even the depths of God...no one comprehends what is truly God's except the Spirit of God" (1 Cor 2:10–11).

For Paul, the Spirit transforms and sanctifies human life. The experience of the Spirit is rooted in the personal transformation of Jesus into the risen Lord and in the personal transformation of Saul the persecutor into Paul the apostle. The presence and power of the Spirit continues in the ongoing life of the community which is God's temple (1 Cor 3:16 17; 6:11,19), enabled to confess Jesus as Lord (1 Cor 12:3; Rom 10:9–12) and to call on his name (Rom 10:13; Acts 2:21), endowed with a variety of spiritual gifts for the benefit of the common good (1 Cor 12:7–13), the greatest of which is love (1 Cor 12:31–13:13; Rom 5:5). Paul began to write letters some eighteen to twenty years after intense apostolic involvement with the communities he founded. Controversies did abound and questions were raised, but Paul could assume a common experiential foundation for Jew and Gentile alike in their cultic devotion to Jesus and in their personal transformation in the Spirit.[24] Paul does not speak of a distinct Pentecostal event such as we have in Acts. Should we understand such an event as part of the originating experience?

James D. G. Dunn offers a good summary of the experience on the day of Pentecost:

> When gathered together in Jerusalem, presumably to await
> the consummation already begun in the resurrection of

Jesus, they were caught up in a communal experience of ecstatic worship which manifested itself particularly in vision and glossalalia. This experience they recognized as the impact of the Spirit of God, and therein they saw the hand of the risen Jesus drawing them together into living community and giving them both impulse and urgency to testify for him.[25]

Dunn argues for an historical event distinct from the resurrection appearances (as listed at 1 Cor 15:3–8), while he recognizes the close connection between such appearances and the mission (Matt 28:18–20) and gift of the Spirit (John 20:21–23) in the Gospels. The sequence of Jesus' death, resurrection, appearances, ascension/exaltation, and giving of the Spirit for mission, so carefully differentiated by Luke, are from a theological perspective distinct dimensions of one unifying event. The dynamic power and guiding agent of these events is the Holy Spirit. Luke's favorite phrase in both the Gospel and Acts is to be "filled with the Holy Spirit." John the Baptist "will be filled with the Holy Spirit" (Luke 1:15), Elizabeth his mother and Zechariah his father were "filled with the Holy Spirit" (1:41, 67), and Jesus begins his mission "full of the Holy Spirit" (4:1). So now, "All of them were filled with the Holy Spirit" (Acts 2:4), a characteristic that applies to Peter (Acts 4:8), to the community (Acts 4:31), to Paul (Acts 9:17; 13:9), and to others. Clearly, the "Acts of the Apostles" would be better termed the "Acts of the Holy Spirit." The Holy Spirit is active and alive, energizing and directing the nascent Church both individually and communally.

While, as Dunn avers, Luke is an "undiscriminating guide" when it comes to the distinctiveness of the experience of the Spirit, some things are notable about his presentation in Acts. First, the Spirit is a free and powerful force like wind and fire that fills and energizes everything, the breadth and length and height and depth, the very fullness of God (cf. Eph 3:14–19). Second, the Spirit is the gift of Jesus (Luke 24:49; Acts 1:4–5, 8; 2:33) so that everything done in the name of Jesus is done in the power of the Spirit. The relationship between the Spirit and baptism is fluid (see Acts 2:38; 8:14–17; 19:2–6) but the quintessential gift was to receive the Holy Spirit. Third, the mission of the apostles cannot succeed unless they are filled and empowered by the Spirit so as to announce with boldness and courage the good news of Jesus' death and resurrection. Fourth, the charismatic gifts given to the community are many and varied but they all serve to establish and build up the Church's life, as in the communal vision that gives rise to an ecstatic speaking in tongues for Jews (2:3–4) and for Gentiles (10:44–48), the power of prophecy given to all in the community (2:17–18, citing Joel 2:28–32), the gifts of wisdom and faith given to those full of the Spirit (6:3–5), the gifts of peace, reverence for the Lord, and comfort (9:31), the gift of joy at experiencing persecution for proclaiming the word of the Lord (13:49–52). Finally, the Spirit gives the leaders of the Church guidance in specific ways (13:2–4; 15:28; 20:28). Strikingly, Paul is characterized as "a captive to the Spirit" who "testifies" to him about his impending persecution (20:22–23). In all of this, the Spirit is seen not merely as an impersonal force or power but as a personal reality who speaks and testifies, as one deeply involved in the future of the Church.

When we turn to the promise of "another Paraclete" in John, we see another reflection of this early Church-inaugurating experience. In the first half of John's Gospel (1—12), the Spirit who "remained on" Jesus at his baptism (1:32) is the Spirit Jesus promises and will give "without measure" (3:34) after his death and resurrection. The words to Nicodemus that everyone must be born of the Spirit anew (3:5–8) are immediately connected to Jesus' first prediction of his death and exaltation (3:14–15). The Samaritan woman is told that the "hour [Jesus' death] is coming, and is now here, when the true worshipers will worship the Father in spirit and truth, for the Father seeks such as these to worship him. God is spirit, and those who worship him must worship in spirit and truth" (4:23–24). Finally, the evangelist makes it explicitly clear that the Spirit will be given to believers only after Jesus' glorification (7:37–39). It is no accident that the "disciple whom Jesus loved" appears for the first time at the beginning of the second half of the Gospel (13—21). He is initially pictured as reclining in the bosom of Jesus (*en tō kolpō tou Iēsous* at 13:23) just as Jesus was initially pictured as being in the bosom of the Father (*ho ōn eis ton kolpon tou patros* at 1:18). As Jesus knows the Father in a deeply intimate way and can therefore reveal him, so the beloved disciple knows Jesus and can reveal who he truly is. He is the true believer but he can only reveal Jesus because he has received "the Spirit of truth" (14:17).

Whether there was actually such an unidentified disciple at the origin of John (see 19:35; 20:31; 21:24), some such deep, personal, interior experience is surely the foundational experience of the Gospel.

Jesus at his death "hands over" the Spirit (19:30), which he breathes into the disciples at the resurrection appearance (20:20; cf. Gen 2:7). The meaning of this in terms of the mission of the disciples (20:21, 23) has already been indicated in five discrete texts during Jesus' farewell discourse: (1) 14:16–17; (2) 14:25–26; (3) 15:26; (4) 16:7–11; (5) 16:12–15. Following the order of Dunn's treatment,[26] there are four points to be made. First, in each of the texts it is clear that this "other" advocate (cf. 1 Jn 2:1) will come to ensure the continuation of Jesus' mission and presence: "he abides with you and he will be in you" (14:17) as do Jesus and the Father (14:23), he will "remind you of all that I have said to you" (14:26), "he will testify on my behalf" (15:26), "he will prove the world wrong…about sin, because they do not believe in me…" (16:8–9), "he will glorify me, because he will take what is mine and declare it to you" (16:14). He is explicitly identified as "the Spirit of truth" (14:17; 15:26; 16:13) because he is the Spirit of Jesus who is "the way, and the truth, and the life" (14:6) and is sent equally by the Father (14:16; 14:26) and by Jesus (15:26; 16:7). The Spirit of truth "comes from the Father" as does Jesus himself, and so Jesus sends him "from the Father" (15:26). Hence, as Dunn indicates, the Spirit will take on the presence and power of Jesus himself after Jesus "goes away" (16:7).

The second point is that the Spirit guarantees the ongoing revelation that maintains both the continuation of the revelation given in Jesus and openness to reinterpretation, a dialectic of continuity that includes identity and difference. Dunn suggests that the author of John would probably consider his own work to be a product of the inspiration of the Spirit, maintaining both continuity with the incarnate Jesus and offering under the guidance of the Spirit—"he will guide you into all the truth…he will take what is mine and declare it to you…" (16:12–15)—the deeper and more profound truth about Jesus (cf. 1 Jn 2:27; 4:2–6; 5:6–10).

The third point is that the context of the religious experience underlying John's Gospel is Spirit-inspired worship. Jesus tells the Samaritan woman at 4:23–24 that true worshipers will worship God the Father, who is Spirit, in Spirit (the Holy Spirit) and truth (Jesus). John's Gospel may not develop the interdependent bonds of community life as does Paul, but the profound communion of the inner-trinitarian life of Father, Son, and Spirit into which each believer is invited is hardly for the individual alone. Indeed, the trinitarian life is the basis for any meaningful sense of community among human beings: "… so that they may be one, as we are one, I in them and you in me, that they may become completely one…" (17:22–23).

The final point, which is the most pertinent for this stage of christological development, is the strong emphasis upon the present experience of Jesus in the power of the Spirit. For John, every believer is a first-generation follower of Jesus because of the faith that is the experience of "eternal life," the term John prefers to "kingdom of God" (cf. 3:3, 5 with 3:15–16, 36; the only other use of kingdom is before Pilate at 19:36 to emphasize that Jesus' kingdom "is not from this world"). This faith is only possible because of the continuing activity of the Spirit in the heart of each believer. Such faith transcends the barrier of death in the present experience of believers. As Jesus tells Martha: "I am the resurrection and the life. Those who believe in me, even though they die, will live, and everyone who lives and believes in me will never die" (11:25–26). The Gospel of John as we have it is the end product of a long and complex period of handing on and refining traditions but, like Paul, it reaches back to the originating events of faith in and devotion to Jesus rooted in the paschal mystery of the Son raised by the Father in the creative and life-giving power of the Spirit.

4. The Anointing of Jesus as God's Son

We turn now to Jesus' "Spirit-filled nature," first from the beginning of his mission as anointed by the Spirit and then, in the next section, from the beginning of his existence as begotten in the power of the Spirit both at his human conception and at his origin in his eternal relation to the Father. "We must repeat emphatically: the whole mystery of the Father is to beget his Son; if therefore the Spirit proceeds from the Father whose whole mystery consists in begetting, and if he himself is not the Son, *he must therefore be this begetting*. Although human language fails us, it would seem that one could say: the Spirit is the action of the Father as father, he is the begetting."[27] Durrwell refers to Irenaeus, who speaks of the Father as the one who anoints, of the Son as the one anointed, and of the Spirit as the unction (or, anointing). We will consider sequentially the Holy Spirit as the anointing and as the begetting, in both cases emphasizing the active character of the Spirit.

In the Synoptic Gospels the Spirit is the source of Jesus' *exousia* (power/authority). When asked by what authority he does these things and who gave him this authority, he responds with a question about the baptism of John (Mark 11:27–33 par). If they had understood that John's baptism came "from heaven," they would have known the source of Jesus' authority. The baptism of Jesus as Mark presents it (Mark 1:9–11) is a revelatory scene that by way of anticipation of the rest of the Gospel communicates the significance of Jesus from God's point of view.[28] Hence, the focus of interest is not simply on the baptism itself (cf. Matt 3:13–17; Luke 3:21–22; John 1:32–34; Acts 10:38), but on what happened immediately after. Only Mark says explicitly that Jesus was baptized by John *into* the Jordan (v. 9) which may be a symbolic anticipation of Jesus' death and resurrection. But the focus is on the sequel structured by a two-step progression that corresponds to the initial claim at 1:1 that Jesus is the Christ, the Son of God: v. 10 is a visual revelation of Jesus as Christ anointed by the Spirit; v. 11 is an auditory revelation of Jesus as the Son of God (Ps 2:7), the beloved Son (Gen 22:2), and the chosen (and beloved at Matt 12:18) servant (Isa 42:1).

Therefore it is God who definitively declares who Jesus is. This is confirmed by an anticipatory "binding of the strong man" (3:27). The triad of being tempted by Satan for forty days, being with the wild beasts, and being served by angels signals the messianic victory, the eschatological age of salvation (cf. Luke 10:18–20). The active agent of its arrival is the Spirit who threw Jesus out (*ekballei*) into the desert (1:12). Matthew and Luke say he was "led by" (Matt 4:1) or "in" (Luke 4:1) the Spirit (in Luke he is characterized as "full of the Holy Spirit"). The fuller accounts of the temptations at Matt 4:1–11 and Luke 4:1–13 make it clear that the struggle with Satan had to do with Jesus' identity as "the Son of God."

The baptismal and temptation narratives are products of early theological insights into Jesus' identity clearly inspired by the Spirit but also rooted in historical memories. Dunn develops Jesus' own religious experience as an experience of sonship and of charismatic empowerment. Jesus knew and prayed to God as "my father" (*abba*) and he went about doing good, healing, preaching, and teaching with power and authority (*exousia*) because anointed by the Spirit.[29] In terms of christological sequence, the early Church would not only have anticipated his return as Son of Man and celebrated his presence and power in the Spirit as Lord and Christ, but would have reflected upon his origins as Son of God. This was surely rooted in their memories of him, of the things he said and did, of the impact he had on their lives, so much so that they always maintained the distinction between his human, historical life culminating in the cross and his exalted, glorified life as risen Lord.

Nonetheless, they interpreted his life in the light of what they now know. They didn't simply remember his words and deeds. They also mined the Hebrew Scriptures to show how his words and deeds, but especially his fate, were the fulfillment of the hopes of Israel. And they did this by focusing on his *personal* identity as revealed by the Spirit of God. If he was declared to be Son of God from the resurrection of the dead (Rom 1:4; Acts 13:33, citing Ps 2:7), then he always was the Son of God empowered by the Holy Spirit from the very beginning of his mission. They also recognized that during his life, and also in their own, the fundamental struggle was between the Spirit and Satan. The demons always knew who he was, the holy one, the Son of God (Mark 1:24, 34; 3:11; 5:7; Matt 4:1–11; Luke 4:1–13). The Spirit anointed him to proclaim good news to the poor and to heal the sick (Luke 4:16–21; Matt 11:2–6 par; Acts 10:36–38), but, above all, to confront the power of Satan (Mark 3:22 27 par). The unforgivable sin is the sin against the Holy Spirit (Mark 3:28–30 par). This is not some imaginable sin in the abstract. It has very concrete and specific reference to Jesus' mission, for the sign that the kingdom of God has come is the fact that he casts out demons by the Spirit (Matt 12:28) or by the finger (Luke 11:20) of God, that is, by the power and authority (*exousia*) of God that he received in his anointing for mission. He gives that same power to his disciples both to share in his mission of healing and preaching (Mark 6:7 par) and to confront future persecution (Mark 13:11 par). In sum, the life and mission of Jesus which he shared with his disciples is understood to be Spirit-empowered and Spirit-guided from beginning to end.

5. The Begetting of Jesus as God's Son

If the tradition of Spirit-inspired theological reflection behind Mark can push Jesus' origins back to the beginning of his mission in the baptism of John, the traditions behind Matthew and Luke push it back to the beginning of his life in the virginal conception. Both, each in his own distinctive way, see Jesus' conception and birth as the fulfillment of Israel's hopes. For this purpose Matthew begins with "the genealogy of Jesus the Messiah, the son of David, the son of Abraham," employs direct citations of biblical texts (Isa 7:14; Mic 5:2; Jer 31:15) to indicate fulfillment of prophetic words, and models his second chapter on the early life of Moses. But central to Matthew's concern is the birth of Jesus without the mediation of a human father: "...before they lived together, she was found to be with child from the Holy Spirit" (Matt 1:18). It is important to note that Joseph knows this only through a revelation. So too the tradition behind Matthew knows this by a deeper reflection upon and interpretation of the revelation that God raised Jesus from the dead, something that could only be known because the Spirit has been guiding them "into all the truth" and so glorifying Jesus (John 16:12–15).

If Matthew's interest is in maintaining the virginal conception, Luke's interest is much more focused on the activity of the Holy Spirit. Luke 1:5–3:22 can be characterized as the 'epoch' of Israel, the rest of the Gospel as the 'epoch' of Jesus, and Acts as the 'epoch' of the Church. But central to all three periods is the activity of the Holy Spirit. The Holy Spirit is tangibly active (*sōmatikō* at 3:22) so that people are frequently described as "filled with the Holy Spirit" (1:15, 41, 67; 2:25–27). Mary and Zechariah both sing the song of Israel, the fulfillment of the promises God made to their ancestors, to Abraham and to his descendants, "to give the knowledge of salvation to his people" (1:77). But central to Luke's concern is the activity of the Holy Spirit in begetting Jesus. "The Holy Spirit will come upon you, and the power of the Most High will overshadow you; therefore the child to be born will be holy; he will be called Son of God" (1:35). The Spirit is not only inspiring prophetic voices but is now creating a new reality. Yet the imagery is trinitarian. The "power of the Most High" (cf. "Son of the Most High" at v. 32) is clearly the power of the God of Israel now identified in Semitic parallelism with the Holy Spirit. The language "will come upon" (*epeleusetai*) and "will cast a shadow over" (*episkiasei*) is figurative. Nonetheless, as Joseph Fitzmyer comments, while the language in and of itself could include a normal human birth, "the step-parallelism in the two announcements [of John and of Jesus] demands that the miraculous divine intervention, precisely invoking the creative power of the Spirit, has to result in a more extraordinary conception, hence, virginal."[30] The point of emphasis, however, is not upon Mary but upon Jesus' origins as the Son of God. As such, the text raises questions about the precise role of the Holy Spirit in the begetting of the Son. If our understanding of the inner-trinitarian life is based on the revelation given to us in Scripture, then this text is of crucial significance for the later theological developments. Before addressing that question, however, we must first complete the analysis of early christological developments back to the beginning of creation.

It is the Gospel of John that most clearly moves Jesus' origins back beyond the created world to the glory he had with the Father "before the world existed" (John 17:5). The Gospel as a whole represents a profound and refined development of Jesus as the Son of God in relation to the Father who sent him and the Spirit who comes from the Father and is sent by the Father and the Son together. The Gospel is rooted in an interior, personal experience of devotion to Jesus as represented by the beloved disciple and it employs earlier christological material, such as the hymn embedded in the prologue (1:1–18). The hymn itself divides into four strophes: 1. (vv. 1–2): the Word (*logos*) in relation to God (*ho theos*); 2. (vv 3–5): the Word in relation to creation/salvation-revelation; 3. (vv 10–12b): the Word in relation to the world (rejection/acceptance); 4. (vv 14, 16): the Word in relation to the community as witness. Thus it celebrates God's creative, revelatory, and salvific activity.[31] The hymn taken by itself does not necessarily connote personal preexistence. It employs the image of the Word (*logos*) which in the Hebrew Scriptures, along with Wisdom and Spirit, is a way of speaking of God's immanence while maintaining the divine transcendence. The imagery of the hymn comes from the Wisdom tradition but there is one striking innovation: "And the Word became flesh and lived among us…" (v 14). As Dunn puts it: "…the revolutionary significance of v. 14 may well be that it marks *not only the transition in the thought of the poem from pre-existence to incarnation, but also the transition from impersonal personification to actual person.*"[32]

The Gospel conflates the image of the Word with the title Son of God so that Jesus is presented throughout as the embodiment of divine wisdom. The long speeches such as John 6:35–50, 51–58 are wisdom discourses. The hymn represents the culminating moment of the divine creative intention. If the Word was "in the beginning" (v. 1, echoing Gen 1:1), now the Word is incarnate (*sarx*), personally embodied in Jesus as the unique Son of the Father. "…and we have seen his glory, the glory as of a father's only son" (*hōs monogenous para patros*). John1:14 affirms, along with 1 Corinthians 8:6; Colossians 1:15–20; Hebrews 1:2b–3c, that Jesus is the person Wisdom became.[33] John's Gospel makes the affirmation much more explicit and unavoidable. However, this hymn along with the other early hymns probably originated in a worship setting inspired by the Spirit to celebrate cultic devotion to Jesus. In the light of the eschatological event of Jesus' death and resurrection, the hymns celebrate the significance of Jesus for the whole of creation from beginning to end.

6. The Cosmic Significance of Jesus

There are six hymns that are thought to have existed in early Christian communities prior to the texts in which they are embedded: Philippians 2:6–11; Colossians 1:15–20; Hebrews 1:2b–3c (as a fragment); 1 Peter 3:18–19, 22 (with interpolations); 1 Timothy 3:16; and John 1:1–18 (with interpolations). Three of the hymns are contrast hymns centered around the eschatological event of Jesus' death and resurrection: the "flesh"/"spirit" contrast in 1 Peter and 1 Timothy (though the latter portrays the earthly side in more epiphanic terms as does the Gospel of John) and the humiliation/exaltation contrast in Philippians.

Whatever one thinks about the preexistence motif at Philippians 2:6, it is clear in the hymn that Jesus' freely given choice to empty himself and enter fully into the Adamic existence under sin, law, and death (*morphēn doulou labōn* at v. 7) and to humble himself by his obedience unto death (v. 8) led to the strongly emphasized consequence (*dio kai* at v. 9) that God the Father (*ho theos*) has highly exalted him and given him *the name* that is above every name.[34] What is striking is that it is now "at the name of Jesus" that the whole of creation should bend the knee and confess "that Jesus Christ is Lord to the glory of God the Father" (vv. 10–11, invoking the strict monotheistic faith of Isa 45:23). It would be hard to find a more strongly worded, concrete expression of Jesus' divinity. He is the object of cosmic worship that includes heaven, earth, and netherworld. He is such because God has "graced him" (*echarisatō autō*) with the divine name so that worship is now inseparably binitarian. The Christian faith remains strongly monotheistic and yet includes Jesus in the worship of the one God. Not only is he worshiped but he is seen as the mediating agent of God's creativity and purpose. In like manner, this is the import of Paul's division of the *Shema Yisrael* (Deut 6:4) so that "God" refers to the Father and "Lord" to Jesus: "...yet for us there is one God, the Father, from whom are all things and for whom we exist, and one Lord, Jesus Christ, through whom are all things and through whom we exist" (1 Cor 8:6). For Paul and for the authors of the early hymns, the experience of God from the beginning to the end of creation includes the experience of Jesus "through whom we exist." This is clearly connected to his mediation of the whole of creation: "through whom are all things."

The hymn at Colossians 1:15–20, which is close to 1 Corinthians 8:6 in content, expresses its cosmic view in two strophes that treat successively protology (vv. 15–18a) and eschatology (vv.18b–20). The key to the hymn lies, however, in the second strophe at v. 18b, which begins somewhat surprisingly with the affirmation that he is the *beginning*, not at creation but as "the firstborn from the dead." The interpretive key lies in the qualifying phrase "in order that he may become in all things preeminent" (*proteuon*; my trans.). Hence, it is the paschal mystery, Jesus' resurrection from the dead elaborated in vv. 19–20 in terms of the fullness (*plēróma*) of God dwelling in him and through him reconciling "all things," that enables the hymn to speak of his comprehensive ("in him," "through him," "for him" at v. 16) preeminence or primacy over the whole of creation in the first strophe. The two strophes interpret each other. The second with its eschatological focus upon Jesus' death and resurrection makes possible the affirmation of his primacy over all creation and the first with its invocation of wisdom imagery interprets the full significance of the resurrection as an eschatological event that embraces the whole of creation from beginning to end. Thus, once again, eschatology leads to and includes protology: the end interprets the beginning and the beginning in turn interprets the end.

Yet we still wait, as did the first Christians, for the eschatological consummation of Christ's reign when he will hand the kingdom over to the Father and God will be "all in all" (1 Cor 15:20–28). As we turn now to the key issues of the doctrinal understanding of the triune God of Scripture, we need to keep in mind that "creation is a finite expression of the infinite Word of God"[35] and that the world God has created is God's own history so that God as Creator is affected and changed as creation moves toward its final fullness.[36] In a word, it is the very nature of God to create, not out of some extrinsic necessity but out of the inner dynamism of divine love expressed in the self-communication of the Word. In this sense, God needs the world in order to be fully and freely who God is as self-communicating love. "Because it is essentially related to God's self-expressive and self-communicative nature as love, the best we can say is that creation expresses God's infinite goodness in a finite way."[37] And it is the Spirit, the giver of life (2 Cor 3:6), who guides us into the proper understanding of tradition as a living and life-giving reality.

CHAPTER THREE

The Triune God of Christian Faith

In the preceding chapter we sought to delineate the experiential basis of the scriptural witness to the triune life of God. Rooted in the paschal mystery, we have explored the whole mystery of Christology as the future coming of Jesus, his presence and power, and his origins. This can be understood horizontally as an emancipatory praxis from creation to eschaton. But inseparably, and more fundamentally, it can be understood as a mystical praxis of entering into the very life of the triune God through the Holy Spirit:

> The pure notion of tradition can then be defined by saying that it is the life of the Holy Spirit in the church, communicating to each member of the body of Christ the faculty of hearing, of receiving, of knowing the truth in the light which belongs to it, and not according to the natural light of human reason. This is true gnosis, owed to an action of the divine light (*phōtismos tēs gnōseōs tēs doksēs tou theou*, 2 Cor 4:6), the unique tradition, independent of all philosophy, independent of all that lives "according to human tradition, according to the elemental spirits of the universe, and not according to Christ" (Col 2:8).[1]

Both approaches inseparably include the fullness of revelation, the comprehensive image of breadth, of the totality as inclusive of both mystical and emancipatory concerns. This is a movement toward all the fullness of God the Father, but one that is mediated by Spirit and Word, distinct but united in a reciprocal relationship. "On the one hand, it is by the Holy Spirit that the Word is made incarnate of the Virgin Mary. On the other hand, it is by the Word, following his incarnation and work of redemption, that the Holy Spirit descends on the members of the church at Pentecost."[2] The Holy Spirit is the agent that makes possible the incarnation, but then it is the incarnate Son who makes possible our sanctification.

As we move from the biblical witness grounded in the mystical experience of worship to a consideration of how that has been understood in reference to the immanent Trinity (following the schema of David Coffey), we will address in this chapter the contextual issues raised in chapter 1, but in reverse order. That is, first we will address the approach and concerns of the Eastern Orthodox; second, the convergence of both East and West around the Holy Spirit as the one who determines "the rules for speaking about God" (Kilian McDonnell); and third, the seemingly more Western concern with the context of evolutionary science as a lens for understanding the final consummation of all things. The focus of trinitarian thinking after Scripture is the ecumenical Creed of Constantinople (381), which is the Church's proclamation (*kērygma*) of the mystery (*dogma*) hidden for all ages and revealed in Christ (Eph 1:3–14).[3] We will center the discussion of the creed around the somewhat differing views of two significant Orthodox theologians, Vladimir Lossky and John Zizioulas. Then, in view of that discussion, we will raise the ecumenical significance of the addition of the *filioque*. Finally, we will explore how and in what sense the eschatological consummation of all things constitutes the inner-trinitarian life. Then, in the fourth chapter, we will return to the two-fold judgment that the economic Trinity that presupposes both the biblical and the immanent Trinity really *is* the reality, both within the divine life and within the divine self-communication to creation.

1. The Ecumenical Creed of Constantinople

Ecumenical sensitivity alone should call all Christians to unite around the original formulation of the creed of 381 and to drop all reference to the *filioque* in liturgical worship.[4] That would be a major step forward but it will not resolve the theological questions, particularly given the Eastern conviction strongly expressed by Vladimir Lossky that with the *filioque* the West has effectively abandoned the common tradition. We reviewed Lossky's position in chapter 1 but now need to bring into focus his main contention, which is shared by the Eastern churches, that the source of our knowledge of the Trinity is not abstract speculation in a philosophical or conceptual mode but the concretely lived experience of liturgical worship inspired and guided by the Holy Spirit—hence the term *mystical theology*.

Orthodox worship has been called "the earthly heaven." The experience enables the faithful to ascend mystically into the very life of the triune God.[5] Lossky, as already noted, combines the apophatic tradition characteristic of Eastern theology with spiritual awareness (*gnōsis pneumatikē*) through the mediation of the Holy Spirit. It is an experience of great joy and great beauty, "one organic, all-embracing and all-transforming act of the whole Church,"[6] an action of the people (*leitourgia*), a "lifting up" (*anaphora*) in which the people ascend with Christ and are transformed so that they see "more deeply into the reality of the world."[7]

Leonid Ouspensky summarizes the use of icons in Orthodox worship that indicates the nature of the experience:

> The men who surrounded Christ saw him only as a man, albeit often as a prophet. For the unbelievers, his divinity is hidden by his form of a servant. For them, the Savior of the world is only a historical figure, the man Jesus. Even his most beloved disciples saw Christ only once in his glorified, deified humanity, and not in the form of a servant; this was before the passion, at the moment of his transfiguration on Mount Tabor. But the church has "eyes to see" just as it has "ears to hear". This is why it hears the Word of God in the Gospel, which is written in human words. Similarly, it always considers Christ through the eyes of an unshakable faith in his divinity. This is why the church depicts him in icons not as an ordinary man, but as the God-man in his glory, even at the moment of his supreme humiliation. Unshakable faith in Christ's divinity is precisely the reason why, in its icons, the Orthodox church never represents him simply as a man who suffers physically, as is the case in Western religious art.[8]

While God the Father cannot be represented, the possibility of representing the God-man in the flesh is contingent upon the confession of Mary as the true mother of God (*theotokos*). The final goal of God's creativity, says Ouspensky, is the transfiguration of creation, the process of deification (*theōsis*) that moves from the creation of humans in the image of God to their re-creation in the likeness of God. This is the eschatological fulfillment realized uniquely in Christ and to be realized for humans in the exercise of their human freedom as open to the transformative power of the Holy Spirit—uniting humans to divine beauty and glory as they are being changed from one degree of glory to another (2 Cor 3:18). "When we attain this goal, we participate in divine life and transform our very nature."[9] In Jesus' transfiguration, he manifested the deified state to which all are called, an experience of the inward light of uncreated grace that brings us into a relationship with each of the divine persons.

Karl Rahner's transcendental anthropology, the openness of the creature to the light of uncreated grace, is, according to John Meyendorff, a return to the "authentic roots" of the patristic tradition. There is an openness of each of the three divine persons (*hypostases*) to the creature that corresponds to the creature's openness to the divine persons. The experiential ground for this is the gift of the Holy Spirit, the love of the triune God poured into our hearts through the Holy Spirit that has been given to us (Rom 5:5). Likewise, it is the Spirit who gives us the power of speech (Acts 2:4, 17) and who determines the rules for speaking about God, how the mystery (*dogma*) comes to expression in proclamation (*kērygma*). How do we understand this Spirit-guided speech in our attempts to articulate in human language the utterly transcendent reality of God? In other words, what is the point of entry for the issues raised in chapter 1 concerning the understanding of person, of the role of each person in the economy and whether those roles correspond to the immanent Trinity, of the importance of the *taxis* (internal order) both within creation and within the divine life, of the related issue of the *filioque*?

Access to the inner-trinitarian life can only be, on the human side, a matter of doxology (praise of God on the basis of the divine deeds or actions), an ecstatic breaking forth of praise and adoration that focuses on God as God. As noted in the introduction, Jürgen Moltmann advocates this in agreement with the Letter to the Ephesians (1:6, 12, 14; 3:20–21). This is, however, a human response that presupposes the divine initiative in communicating God's own Self to us. Given that the divine nature or essence is absolutely transcendent and incomprehensible, God employs manifestations ("energies") to communicate with us, according to Lossky and the Orthodox tradition. Moses on Sinai and Jesus on Tabor would be instances of divine energies manifest in luminous ways. The energies are the uncreated outpourings of the inaccessible divine essence. They include the communications of divine grace that enable us to become divinized. But if the energies are inseparable from the nature ("natural processions" says Lossky), the nature is inseparable from the three persons (*hypostases*). The revelation of the triune life of God as Father-Son-Spirit is the primordial "given" of Christian faith. It cannot be deduced from the divine essence, which is inaccessible and incomprehensible. Given the apophatic assumption characteristic of Eastern theology, and the overriding emphasis on "the supremely practical" goal of ascent to mystical union with the divine (*theōsis*), how can we speak at all of the inner-trinitarian relations? Yet, we do have language that, while more confessional than conceptual, does communicate meaning and make affirmations.

That language is hypostatic, the *henōsis kath' hypostasin* of Cyril of Alexandria and the Council of Ephesus (431). According to John Zizioulas, the patristic tradition and especially the Cappadocians created an "ontological revolution" by identifying ontological being (*hypostasis*) with person (*prosōpon*). As a consequence, *hypostasis* had to be differentiated from *ousia* (being as substance or essence), as in the trinitarian formula: one *ousia* and three *prosōpa* (*hypostases*). What this did was create an ontology of personhood in which relational experiences of otherness, difference, relatedness, and communion were perceived as ontological realities and not as accidental additions to the more fundamental reality of essence or substance, as in the Greek philosophical view. This development assumes the prior and early eucharistic consciousness, as in Ignatius of Antioch and Irenaeus, of ecclesial communion, that is, the ontological constitution of the Body of Christ (the Church) through the eschatological fulfillment of history in the Holy Spirit. Hence, Zizioulas affirms that we do have access to and so knowledge of the immanent Trinity.

How does this view of divine personhood relate to Lossky's view of divine energies? And, in what sense does Zizioulas affirm the apophatic emphasis traditional to Eastern Orthodoxy? In a valuable article that clarifies the views of both Lossky and Zizioulas, Aristotle Papanikolaou affirms:

> It must first be remembered that Zizioulas himself is not negating the importance of apophaticism for theology, but affirming the priority of ontology over apophaticism. Zizioulas's contribution lies in providing the means to link apophaticism and ontology within trinitarian reflection. In this sense, his thought is not so much a rejection of Lossky's as it is a completion.[10]

The issue is how to conceive the immanence and transcendence of God, how *realistically* we can take the communion between the divine and the human. As we have seen, Lossky emphasizes apophaticism and the "energies" of God. The distinction is between God's essence as transcendent that ensures the absolute freedom of God and the divine "energies" as immanent that preserves the integrity of created existence. "The Incarnation is the event of real communion, such that the created human nature in Christ is deified through participation in God's life. This participation is in God's energies, which is to be distinguished from God's essence."[11]

Lossky's method is "antinomic" in character. Eschewing all attempts at rational conceptualization in favor of the mystical experience in faith, he can maintain two realities that are logically inconsistent and cannot be grasped by reason, but are equally true. "The plea here is that the theologian in search of the God of Christian revelation, who transcends the opposition between the transcendent and the immanent, since he is beyond all affirmation and all negation, be directed 'even beyond unknowing' and toward the way of union with triune Divinity."[12] Hence, Lossky affirms in the same article a dialectic of the "non-opposition of opposites" so that one can affirm as equally true the unity of the divine nature and the diversity of the divine persons without giving primacy to the *hypostases* over the *ousia* or vice versa. The attempt to rationalize the dogma of the Trinity (as in the Western *filioque*) "suppresses the fundamental antinomy between the essence and the hypostases...the primordial antinomy of absolute identity and no less absolute diversity in God...." Unlike the Anselmian approach of faith seeking understanding that seeks to explain revelation with the use of philosophical concepts, in the apophatic approach "…understanding seeks the realities of faith, in order to be transformed by becoming more and more open to the mysteries of revelation."[13]

For Zizioulas on the other hand: "Apophaticism is no longer foundational in God-talk, while person replaces energies as the dominant soteriological concept."[14] Apophaticism is qualified by affirming in the Rahnerian sense that the immanent Trinity *is* the economic Trinity—the experience of God in history tells us who God is—but the economic Trinity does not exhaust the divine essence (*ousia*) because God is essentially unknowable. Hence, apophaticism is affirmed in reference to *the what* of God's existence. Also, the divine energies are qualified in that the energies always flow from the person and, secondly, that "…salvation is not described for Zizioulas as an increase in participation in the divine energies, but as the transformation of being into true personhood *in* the person of Christ."[15]

"Zizioulas transcends the Losskian dialectic between apophaticism and rationalism by rooting theology in the liturgical experience of God."[16] While maintaining the Cappadocian distinction between the essence (*ousia*) of God which is unknowable and the mode or manner of God's being (*tropos hyparcheōs*), he maintains that in the incarnate Christ God has revealed the latter as the immanent trinitarian life. The foundational experience that makes the Trinity knowable is the trinitarian worship of the eucharistic liturgy in which the incarnate Christ is made present and known in his hypostatic or personal existence. Zizioulas is not arguing for an ontology based on the *ousia* of God but on the personhood (*hypostasis*) of God as triune. How one knows this God is not lost in the lithophanic eternity of God's essence, but is communicated in the liturgical worship of Father, Son, and Spirit. What then is the "role" of each person as manifested both biblically and liturgically? While following the usual order of Father, Son, and Spirit, we acknowledge with Zizioulas that the Trinity is a primordial datum of faith so that one cannot talk about the being of God apart from the relational reality of communion.[17]

The cause (*aitia*) of this communion is the *person* of the Father. "This thesis of the Cappadocians that introduced the concept of 'cause' into the being of God assumed an incalculable importance. For it meant that the ultimate ontological category which makes something really *be*, is neither an impersonal and incommunicable 'substance', nor a structure of communion existing by itself or imposed by necessity, but rather the *person*."[18] Zizioulas speaks of two basic "leavenings" of Greek thought by the Church Fathers. The first, based on creation *ex nihilo*, turned the existence of the world from a matter of necessity to a product of freedom. But, more profoundly, the second identified the very being of God with the person of the Father who in his personal freedom, out of love, begets the Son and brings forth the Spirit because he freely wills to exist as Father. "Thus God as person—as the hypostasis of the Father—makes the one divine substance to be that which it is: the one God. This point is absolutely crucial.... Outside the Trinity there is no God, that is, no divine substance, because the ontological 'principle' of God is the Father. The personal existence of God (the Father) constitutes His substance, makes it hypostases. The being of God is identified with the person."[19]

Not only does the Father freely will the creation but he freely wills this communion of persons. The Greek insistence on necessity is shattered on the personal reality of the Father who, as "absolute ontological freedom," is unbounded by any necessity and unites all things, including the divine life, in the only authentic and true freedom. The freedom of Christ, and the freedom that constitutes our salvation, is complete and total union with the gift of the Father's love. "The life of God is eternal because it is personal, that is to say, it is realized as an expression of free communion, as love."[20] This love endows each person with uniqueness, with a name that symbolizes a concrete, unique, unrepeatable identity.

Salvation, the process of divinization (*theōsis*), comes through the fully human one, the Christ who incarnates the fullness of human personhood precisely because of his hypostatic unity with the divine. This is made present and effective for us through the paschal mystery celebrated in the Eucharist. "The fact that *finally* death is conquered gives us the right to believe that the conqueror of death was also *originally* God. This is the way Christology in the New Testament has developed—from the resurrection to the incarnation, not the other way round—and patristic theology has never lost this eschatological approach to Christology."[21] The person of Christ is "ontologically true" because only in him do being (truth) and life (communion) coincide. He is the revelation of true personhood, not just as an individual who died for us in an ethical or psychological sense; he is a true person because he was raised as the *ontological* truth.

In discussing the relationship between Christology and pneumatology, Zizioulas sees a dialectic between the mission of the Son and the mission of the Spirit.[22] Only the Son *becomes* history; the Spirit brings into history the *eschaton*. "The Spirit makes of Christ an eschatological being, the 'last Adam'."[23] The Spirit makes Christ "a corporate personality," and so makes the Church exist above all in the eschatological experience of the Eucharist. Thus, in the Son's mission, pneumatology is conditioned by Christology. This is the "historical approach" that provides the structure of apostolic continuity. The Spirit is sent by Christ to empower the apostles for their mission to the ends of the earth (Acts 1:8). The Spirit is the agent of Christ and is dependent upon him. On the other hand, in the Spirit's mission, Christology is conditioned by pneumatology. This is the "eschatological approach" whereby "the Spirit is the one who brings the eschaton into history" (Acts 2:17). "...the Spirit is 'the Lord' who transcends linear history and turns historical continuity into a presence." The two approaches are united in fact into one synthesis in the Eucharist.[24]

Zizioulas has a longer treatment of the ecclesiological implications of his view, but for our purposes the important point is that the Body of Christ, the Church, is formed in the Spirit as the ontological reality of the Christ-event. In the Spirit, Christ and Church are one. The Eucharist is the quintessential experience of truth as communion, not truth as rational or even mystical but ontological truth as a communion-event created by the Spirit. "Academic theology may concern itself with doctrine, but it is the communion of the Church that makes theology into truth."[25] When the Spirit makes the eschaton present in the person of Christ, this is the actualization and fulfillment of history. It took place in the resurrection and it takes place when the Church, in celebrating the mysteries, ascends to the Father.

Based on the biblical and liturgical experience of the triune life as an ontologically real communion of the divine and the human in Christ[26] and based on the pervasive activity of the Holy Spirit in the life of Christ and in the life of the Church, both of which reveal truth about the inner life of God, how then are we to understand the claim that the Father begets the Son and brings forth the Spirit? In what sense do the Son and the Spirit relate to each other in the dynamic unfolding of the divine life? This brings us to the question of the *filioque*.

2. The Addition of *filioque*: Orthodox or Heretical?

"Whether we like it or not, the question of the procession of the Holy Spirit has been the sole dogmatic grounds for the separation of East and West."[27] Lossky is so insistent upon this fact because he views the two formulae—"from the Father alone" (*ek monou tou patros*) and "from the Father and the Son as from one principle" (*a patre filioque tanquam ab uno principio*)—as representing two diametrically opposed *traditions*, or perhaps better put, "the pure notion of tradition" comes in the Orthodox view from the light, that is, the experience of the Holy Spirit. The *filioque*, as a later interpolation to the original creed, cannot lay claim to that. He recognizes that there has been imprecision and obscurity in the description of the Holy Spirit (e.g., procession vs. generation), but to consider the Holy Spirit as a merely passive recipient of the "relation of opposition" between Father and Son renders even more obscure the distinct identity of the Spirit as a *hypostasis*. By way of contrast, the Orthodox appeal to "relations of origin" because the basis for the hypostases is not the relations as such. The Father, the "mode of origin" or "mode of subsistence" (*tropos hyparcheōs*), alone determines their absolute diversity. "Here it may be stated that the relations serve only to *express* the hypostatic diversity of the three; they are not the basis of it. It is the absolute diversity of the three hypostases which determines their differing relations to one another, not vice versa."[28] At this point, Lossky refers to his antinomic method as treated above. He sees here a complete divergence in the two ways of doing *theologia*, so that the term seems to be equivocal.

Lossky is concerned to affirm the essential identity of the three divine persons, their consubstantiality, but their unity is inconceivable apart from the monarchy of the Father who is the *principle* or *cause* of the one essence that is common to all three. "There is neither an impersonal substance nor nonconsubstantial persons. The one nature and the three hypostases are presented simultaneously to our understanding, with neither prior to the other. The origin of the hypostases is not impersonal, since it is referred to the person of the Father; but it is unthinkable apart from their common possession of the same essence, the 'divinity in division undivided'."[29] The Father is appropriately so called because he is not the essence of God but a person who causes the other consubstantial persons to have the same essence. It is the threefold character of God in absolute diversity that prevents the collapse of the triunity into a simplicity of essence, as is seen in the Western tendency toward modalism. On the other hand, it is the personal character of the Father as cause who prevents any Eastern tendency to subordinationism because the perfect cause produces effects of equality, not inferiority.

In turning to the divine "manifestations" or revelation in the economy, Lossky again affirms the absolute unknowability of the divine essence and the divine energies as manifestations of that same essence. Consistent with this, he makes an interesting statement on the order (*taxis*) of the persons:

> In the order of divine manifestation, the hypostases are not the respective images of the personal diversities but of the common nature: The Father reveals his nature through the Son, and the divinity of the Son is manifested in the Holy Spirit. This is why, in the realm of divine manifestation, it is possible to establish an order of persons (*taxis*) which, strictly speaking, should not be attributed to trinitarian existence in itself, despite the monarchy and causality of the Father. These confer upon him no hypostatic primacy over the other two hypostases, since he is a person only because the Son and the Holy Spirit are also.[30]

But, is the order of the Son preceding the Spirit that clear in the economy? Many authors today, both East and West, recognize the priority of the Spirit who "rests upon" Jesus in his conception, his baptism, and his historical mission, which is especially clear in Luke's Gospel as analyzed in chapter 2. They appeal to such language as mutual interdependence, reciprocity, mutuality. However that issue is resolved, if there is to be any East–West dialogue on the Trinity, the absolute priority of the Father must be maintained. The Father, by reason of his own unique character as a hypostasis, which he does not communicate to the Son and the Spirit, is the origin, the cause, the source of the distinct personhood of the Trinity. He is a person, as Lossky says, because the Son and the Holy Spirit are persons also.

But, in considering the relationship of Son and Spirit, there is a movement of reciprocity that reflects the inner-trinitarian life. To cite Boris Bobrinskoy:

> It is from this ecclesial, sacramental, spiritual experience of Christ, who is anointed by the Holy Spirit (Luke 4:4, 14, 18; Acts 2:33), and of his Body, the Church, herself the bearer of the Spirit, that theological vision attains to the intuition of the eternal mystery of the Holy Spirit, no longer as proceeding from the Son, or through the Son, but as resting on the Son from all eternity. The descent of the Spirit on Jesus at the Jordan therefore appears in the Orthodox trinitarian vision as an icon, a manifestation in history of the eternal resting of the Spirit of the Father on the Son. Thus it is that, following St. John Damascene, the Orthodox liturgy for Pentecost proclaims, "the Spirit who proceeds from the Father and rests on the Son".[31]

On the Western side, Thomas Smail offers a clear summary of the controversy between East and West. The strength of the Eastern position is the strong emphasis on the primacy of the Father, while its weakness is the lack of a clear view on the relation of the Spirit and the Son. The strength of the Western position is that it anchors pneumatology in Christology, the Spirit is clearly the Spirit of the Son, while its weakness is that the Spirit does not seem to be on the same level as the Father and Son insofar as the Spirit has no part in bringing forth a divine person as does the Son. The Western position is too Christ-centered and downplays the role of the Spirit both in the inner life of God and in the Church. As a possible solution, Smail proposes a mutual interdependence of the Spirit and the Son with their ultimate source in the Father. It is a relationship "of coordination rather than subordination." He says that, in faithfulness to the biblical data, we may need not one but two alterations to the creed of 381 (at least in its interpretation if not its formulation since the citation of John 15:26 does not of itself resolve the subsequent theological questions). The third article on the Spirit should affirm that "the Spirit proceeds from the Father *through the Son*" (citing Gregory of Nyssa), while the second article on the Son should affirm that the Son "is eternally begotten of the Father *through the Spirit*."[32]

Both affirmations are based on the biblical data and the ecclesial experience, especially in the liturgy, of the mutual and interdependent relations of the Spirit and the Son. We will return to this proposal in the next chapter as it effectively eliminates the language of *filioque* and offers an alternative that is close to the three models we will examine. Prior to that, however, there is one further question that needs to be discussed in the light of Eastern and Western approaches to the divine mystery, the relationship between time and eternity as it affects the inner-trinitarian life.

3. The Eschatological Consummation of the Trinitarian Life

The Spirit is the dynamic presence and power of God not only in the Church but in the whole cosmos. If the Spirit makes the eschaton present in the person of the risen Christ and constitutes the Church ontologically as such, especially in its liturgical celebrations, then we must acknowledge also that this experience does not isolate or remove us from the ongoing processes of history but drives us more deeply into history and the world as the locus of God's self-communication. All true mystical experience allows us to see more deeply into the reality of the world, as Alexander Schmemann says. And nowhere is this more evident than in the personal experience of Jesus on the cross. Time and eternity intersect at this particular moment. Indeed with the incarnation, the Word *become* flesh (John 1:14), time has changed its meaning from *chronos* to *kairos*: "The time has been fulfilled" (*ho kairos peplērotai* at Mark 1:15). If the Spirit makes present the *eschaton*, it is Christ who has become history as the Father's eternal self-communication now expressed in the otherness and particularity of the temporal process. On the other hand, it is Christ who unites our humanity with the divine in the eschatological event of the resurrection, while it is the Spirit who multiplies that possibility in the distinctness and otherness of our human lives and histories.

All of this is predicated on freedom: the freedom of God in creating and the freedom of humans in responding to the divine initiative. But freedom entails responsibility: the responsibility of God and the responsibility of ourselves as cooperating with God in the building of the earth, in the transformation of the world through the power of God's love on the cross where Jesus "handed over the Spirit" (John 19:30). While the horizons of evolutionary science in an emergent universe remain fundamental to our understanding of the future, we must agree with Jürgen Moltmann that evolution has victims of its own, as does history. Only through the resurrection of nature can the victims of evolution experience justice. "If Christ is to be thought of in conjunction with evolution, he must become evolution's redeemer."[33] Thus, Moltmann distinguishes between "Christ in his becoming" (Christ as "the way" moving the process of evolution forward) and "Christ in his coming" (Christ as the redeemer of nature, including the whole cosmos). However, must the *novum* be absolutely new, a new creation, so that redemption in Christ is counter to evolution, or should it be conceived as the renewal of all things in Christ, so that God's creative activity is continuous with all that has preceded from creation to covenant to incarnation?

All the fullness of God (Eph 3:19) must include at one and the same time the mystical praxis (the vertical height and depth) that seeks to transcend time and space, and the emancipatory praxis (the horizontal length from beginning to end) that seeks the full and final liberation of all God's children, including nature (Rom 8:18–25). Both are embraced and enfolded in the comprehensive breadth of the divine *plērōma*. It is not a question of opposing the temporal and the eternal, the finite and the infinite, for the creative activity of God has involved the very life of God in the creative process. God exists as triune in a different way. "For in him [Christ] the whole fullness of deity dwells [present tense] bodily, and you have come to fullness in him, who is the head of every ruler and authority" (Col 2:9–10). Both Colossians and Ephesians emphasize the Church as the privileged place of the divine *plērōma*. "And he has put all things under his feet and has made him the head over all things for the church, which is his body, the fullness of him who fills all in all" (Eph 1:22–23; cf. 4:7–16). But God's will, set forth in Christ, is "a plan for the fullness of time, to gather up all things in him, things in heaven and things on earth" (Eph 1:10).

From the biblical perspective, God's personal self-communication and self-involvement in the creative process includes both time and eternity, so that God is always intimately present to every particle in the uni-

verse and is calling forth new possibilities, with the intention that finally
the entire universe will be transformed by the eternal embrace of God and
God the Father will be "all in all" (1 Cor 15:28). It is important to note
again (see the introduction) that Scripture always maintains the absolute
transcendence and the complete immanence of God. Only then can there
be a *realistic* assessment of God's self-communication to us, that it is truly
God who communicates and it is truly a *human* response that receives the
communication. God dwells with us (Emmanuel) *bodily* in Christ and in
the Church. The fullness of God cannot be divorced, therefore, from the
concrete and specific process of history and of the cosmos.

Time as well as eternity is a great mystery, just as human freedom is
in relation to divine freedom. "God is eternal because he has no future
outside himself. His future is that of himself and of all that is distinct from
him. But to have no future outside oneself, to be one's own future, is perfect freedom. The eternal God as the absolute future, in the fellowship of
Father, Son, and Spirit, is the free origin of himself and his creatures."[34]

Whereas God has within the divine Self the end (the future) that
constitutes God, we can have that future only in God. Thus eternity is not
opposed to time but relates to it positively and embraces it in its totality,
which will come in the eschatological consummation of the trinitarian
life. The concrete reality of that life is revealed in God's specific acts in history.[35] "Because God is love, having once created a world in his freedom,
he finally does not have his own existence without this world, but over
against it and in it in the process of its ongoing consummation."[36] Ted
Peters, commenting on Pannenberg's use of Plotinus, affirms Pannenberg
but not Plotinus: "The eternity in which we place our hope consists in the
integration of parts and whole and the consummation of temporal history,
not in their virtual annihilation into an ever present now."[37] This entails
the "holistic principle" of science as applied to theology. The whole is
greater than the parts because a higher system of organization or order
sublates the lower, while maintaining the validity of each level, into a
more complex configuration. For example, there are increasing levels of
complexity as nature moves from the physical to the chemical to the biological to the reflectively conscious levels:

> Yet, whereas in the scientific model the parts are present
> within the whole and exhaust the physical being of the
> whole, in trinitarian theology we want to add that the whole

67

is also present among the parts. In the incarnation of Jesus Christ, the whole is present as one part among others. The eternal has become temporal. The infinite has become finite. And the work of the Holy Spirit anticipatorily binds the part to the whole, the present to the future, the expectation to its fulfillment.[38]

The death and resurrection of Jesus is the proleptic anticipation of God's future because Jesus as the risen Christ constitutes ontologically the final transformation of the whole of creation. Yet, he does this precisely as a human so that the particularity and temporality of human experience is constitutive of the divine experience. God's creative initiative transforms the world *from within*, mediated by Jesus' human freedom (Phil 2:6–8; 1 Tim 2:5), so that now the risen Christ must reign until he hands the kingdom over to the Father (1 Cor 15:24). God's promised future in the resurrection is that nothing in all creation that is true, nothing that is good, nothing that is beautiful will ever be lost but that all will be transformed in the one who is all (1 Cor 15:28).

As we move from this chapter to the next, we are asking how all this affects the triune God of Christian faith. Does the Eastern perspective that we have been emphasizing connect with the Western views that we now propose? Without changing the wording of the ecumenical creed of 381, is it time to acknowledge that both East and West have engaged in theological interpretations of the original text such that a convergence of views may now be possible?

CHAPTER FOUR

Ecumenical Overture:
Three Views from the West

What we need today is a trinitarian Christology. On the level of the economic Trinity, we have been emphasizing the experience of the Son and of the Spirit as an experience of the divine reality expressed in both the scriptural witness and the subsequent liturgical celebrations. This experience raises questions for understanding and inspires a search for adequate conceptualizations. The foundational link for the move from experience to judgment is the understanding of *person*. Normally, we understand a person to be a distinct center of activity who experiences a sense of personal identity as mediated primarily through social relationships. That is, a person as relational can be in another while remaining oneself but a person can only be oneself in the other. The human experience of trust is an act of self-transcendence without which one cannot truly be a person. We can understand by analogy that the very nature of God as love is an active self-communication through self-transcendence (*ek-stasis*). The Spirit is the agent of that relationship within the divine life and within ourselves, but the Father is the source or cause of that relational reality by bringing forth the Spirit and generating the Son. How closely then can we affirm the Spirit's active role in the begetting of the Son? If, as F. X. Durrwell says, the whole mystery of the Father is to beget the Son, and the Spirit who is not the Son proceeds from the Father, then in some sense, as witnessed in Jesus' baptism and conception, the Spirit is not only this anointing but also this begetting.

If the experience of the triune life in worship, as mediated by Scripture and Liturgy, is one of mutual interaction, then the judgment would follow that this is the case in the inner-trinitarian life as well as in the economy. Nonetheless, we must heed the caution of Walter Kasper that we cannot simply transfer our experience of personhood to the inner-trinitarian life. While we can accept a "unity of conscious-ness," with Karl Barth and Karl Rahner, we cannot accept "three con-sciousnesses" in God. However, we must affirm three centers (subjects) of consciousness and action. "…in the Trinity we are dealing with three subjects who are reciprocally conscious of each other by reason of one and the same consciousness which the three subjects 'possess', each in his own proper way."[1] The Trinity is a perichoretic unity of conscious-ness in which each is supremely active in relation to the other two. The essence or nature of God is a communion of persons who are by that fact intensely interrelational and hence supremely dialogical.[2]

The present chapter proposes three models derived from three contemporary Western theologians that raise the question in each case of what exactly we are affirming in our theological judgment. Clearly, each author disagrees on some of the fundamental issues, yet the three together do offer perspectives essential to an adequate trinitarian Christology. The question we are pursuing is framed well by Kasper. At the conclusion of his discussion of the different theologies in East and West regarding the Holy Spirit, he avers: "The ultimate question that waits in the background is that of the relation between the activity of the Holy Spirit in the economy of salvation as the Spirit of Jesus Christ, and the being of the Spirit within the Trinity. A dialogue on the differ-ent formulas of the past must be conducted with an openness to the future, in order to bring clarification to the still unresolved problems on both sides."[3] We have considered the views of some Eastern the-ologians. Now let us consider three views from the West in the inter-ests of furthering the ecumenical dialogue.

1. Jürgen Moltmann: A "Social" Model

Theology, as Walter Kasper puts it, is about "the Godness of God." Soteriology (focus on the human) as he says must pass over into doxol-ogy (focus on God).[4] This is certainly true of Moltmann who along with Kasper sees the doctrine of the Trinity as "the distinctive feature of Christianity" which cannot be relativized.[5] Moltmann advocates a "social doctrine of the Trinity" based in the relational mutuality or peri-choretic unity of the inner divine life which at the same time is "the model for a just and livable community in the world of nature and human beings."[6] Indeed, he opposes any attempt to separate the world from God. Everything that happens in the world happens in God. He has, as he says, "replaced the metaphysical axiom of the essential impassibility of the divine nature with the essential passion of the eternal love of God...."[7] One cannot argue from the economic Trinity to the immanent Trinity but one can experience the immanent Trinity as inherent in our faith experience empowered by the Holy Spirit. This transcends the attempt to deduce the personhood of the Holy Spirit from the Spirit's effects on us and, "in doxological ecstasy," calls one to enter into the interpersonal relationships of Father, Son, and Spirit. "The essential nature of the Holy Spirit is evident only in his interpersonal relationships with the Father and the Son in the trinitarian unity, because only they are of 'like nature'. Their trinitarian inter-subjectivity illuminates the subjectivity of the Holy Spirit. Their trinitarian community illuminates the personhood of the Holy Spirit. The Spirit's personhood is constituted by his interrelatedness with the Father and the Son."[8]

Moltmann's starting point for "trinitarian *thinking*" (as well as doctrine) is the "trinitarian history" that necessitates "narrative differentiation."[9] He states this clearly in his opening to *The Trinity and the Kingdom*:

> The present book is an attempt to start with the special Christian tradition of the history of Jesus the Son, and from that to develop a historical doctrine of the Trinity....In distinction to the trinity of substance and to the trinity of subject we shall be attempting to develop a social doctrine of the Trinity. We understand the scriptures as the testimony to the history of the Trinity's relations of fellowship, which are open to men and women, and open to the world.[10]

Thus, he emphasizes repeatedly that the experiential basis for the triune life is the interaction and relationship of the three as "subjects" who are each unique. This is clear in the relation of Father and Son, as seen in Jesus' prayer to the Father in Gethsemane, but is more problematic, at least in traditional theology, in the case of the Holy Spirit. "Is the Holy Spirit the subject of acts affecting the Son and the Father? For it is only in this sense that it would be justifiable to call the Holy Spirit a divine person."[11] He goes on to say that the Spirit is the *subject* who glorifies the risen Lord and through him the Father and so unites the Son with the Father and the Father with the Son.

Moltmann's strength here is that he sees each of the persons as a unique center of activity within the history of the world and correspondingly within the inner divine life and yet sees these activities as inseparably trinitarian. Thus the creation of the Father is a "trinitarian creation," the incarnation of the Son is a "trinitarian incarnation," and the transfiguration of the Spirit is a "trinitarian glorification." Everything is rooted in the affirmation that God is love, which is true of the triune life as such, yet is affirmed of each person in a unique way. With respect to the triune life as such: "God's freedom can never contradict the truth which he himself is...if God is love, and if he reveals his being in the delivering up of his Son, is he conceivable at all as not-love? Can God really be content to be sufficient for himself if he *is* love?"[12]

With respect to the uniqueness of each person and especially the personhood of the Holy Spirit, Moltmann rejects any form of "monotheistic monarchianism" as found in the subordinationism of Arius and in the modalism of Sabellius. He also rejects the more refined "trinitarian monarchy" of Barth's "modes of being" and Rahner's "modes of subsistence" that attempt to replace the absolute substance with the absolute subject. Commenting on Barth's view of the Holy Spirit as the love between the two "modes of being" of Father and Son, he says:

> The God who reveals himself in three modes of being can no longer display subjectivity in his state-of-revelation, the Holy Spirit. The Spirit is merely the common bond of love linking the Father with the Son....In order to think of their mutual relationship as love, there is no need for a third Person in the Trinity. If the Spirit is only termed the unity of what is separated, then he loses every centre of activity. He is then an energy but not a Person. He is then a relationship but not a subject. Basically, the reflection *Trinity of the absolute subject* is a duality. [13]

The tradition affirms that the Holy Spirit is a distinct person in the Trinity and not merely a functional correlation. If we follow the biblical testimony of the three persons in history, on the other hand, it makes the unity of God a problem that can only be resolved at the eschatological consummation of the trinitarian history. "The unity of the three Persons of this history must consequently be understood as a *communicable* unity and as an *open, inviting unity, capable of integration.*"[14] This unity must not be conceived as "the homogeneity of the one divine substance" or as "the identity of the absolute subject" or as identified with one of the three Persons, but as a "perichoretic unity" of "at-oneness" or "unitedness."[15]

Moltmann affirms with a vengeance Rahner's axiom that the economic Trinity is the immanent Trinity and vice versa. This is so because he sees the cross as an event within the divine life and so does not separate the history of salvation from doxological experience. "It follows from this interlacing of the doctrine of salvation with doxology that we may not assume anything as existing in God himself which contradicts the history of salvation; and, conversely, may not assume anything in the experience of salvation which does not have its foundation in God."[16] He frequently employs four "conceptual frameworks," or models, to articulate the grammar of trinitarian thinking: "the monarchical concept," "eschatological process," "the eucharistic concept," and "trinitarian doxology," the last of which gives us the true access to the immanent Trinity because it reveals the full personhood of the Holy Spirit. That is, the first three models, which reflect the economic Trinity, are completed and subsumed into the doxological statement of the creed: "who *together with* the Father and Son is worshipped and glorified." "Worship and glorification go beyond the salvation that has been experienced and also beyond the thanksgiving that has been expressed. The triune God is glorified for God's own sake. The trinitarian doxology is the only place in the Christian liturgy and life in which—at least in intention—our gaze passes beyond history to the eternal essence of God in himself, so that here we can talk about a doctrine of the 'immanent Trinity'."[17] He describes this experience in terms of ecstasy, a momentary awareness of eternity, that sees the Spirit in "perichoretic fellowship" with the Father and the Son in the dynamic interaction of "self-circling and self-reposing."[18]

In this connection, Moltmann raises the question of the *filioque*. His complete formulation as an interpretation of the text of the creed is as follows: "*The Holy Spirit who proceeds from the Father of the Son, and receives his form from the Father and from the Son.*"[19] He makes a distinction between the constitution of the Trinity and the Trinity's inner life. The Father as unoriginate origin constitutes the Son and the Spirit. He is always and inseparably the Father of the Son. This is the true meaning of the appellation "Father" (vs. any monarchical view, that is, Father, Son, Spirit are *theological* categories, not cosmological, political, or even religious). "The Father is in eternity solely the Father of the Son. He is not the Father of the Spirit. The procession of the Spirit from the Father therefore presupposes the eternal begetting of the Son by the Father, for it is only in it that the Father is and is shown to be the Father." The Spirit's procession then "presupposes (1) the generation of the Son, (2) the existence of the Son, and (3) the mutual relation of the Father and the Son." In summary: "Our proposal is this: the Holy Spirit receives from the Father his own perfect divine existence (*hypostasis, hyparksis*), and obtains from the Son his relational form (*Gestalt*) (*eidos, prosōpon*)."[20] With the Eastern tradition, he maintains that the Spirit proceeds from the Father "alone" in the sense of proceeding but, with the Western tradition, he maintains that the *filioque* has its proper place in regard to the relational form. He is speaking here of the Spirit's proper role as a person to manifest the glory of the Father and the Son and so unite them in the eternal and aesthetic experience of beauty, which he calls "bliss."

Again, this is a social doctrine of the Trinity. The eternal perichoresis plays itself out in the trinitarian history of salvation which moves toward the reception and unification of the whole of creation. The history of salvation "is the love story of God whose very life is the eternal process of engendering, responding, and blissful love."[21] Moltmann is not thinking of three individuals who subsequently enter into relationship as in tritheism nor of three modes or repetitions as in modalism, but of a perichoretic unity in the circulation of the divine life. The Father is engendering love, the Son is responsive love, and the Spirit is blissful love. That is, the Spirit is not the bond of love (as in Augustine) because the Father and Son already love each other. The Spirit "ek-sists *in*" their mutual love as a distinct *person* who illumines or glorifies the Father and the Son. "If we call God the Father the origin of the *divine Being* of the Son and the Spirit, we may see the Son as the origin of the *divine Love* of the Father and the Spirit, and the Holy Spirit as the origin of the *divine Light* which illuminated the Father and the Son. In the complete harmony of Being, Love, and Light we may recognize the *full Joy* and the *perfect Bliss* of the Trinity."[22]

In this perichoresis, there can be no Son without the Spirit and no Spirit without the Son. The persons, their relations, and the changes in history must be thought *together*. But each of the persons takes on a distinctive role in relation to the others as seen in their distinctive names: "*Father*" in relation to the Son and "*Producer*" (*proboleus*) in relation to the Spirit; "*Son*" in relation to the Father and "*Word*" in relation to the Spirit; "*Spirit*" in relation to the Father and "*Light*" in relation to the Son. "Each Person unites and distinguishes the two others through their different relationships to each other....Because every Person and every relationship in the Trinity is unique, one must not speak of a 'filioque' and one should also drop the idea of the Father as the 'monarche' of the Son and the Spirit."[23] With the East, the Father is the sole origin of the Spirit and, with the West, the Son is active in the Spirit's reception of form within the perichoretic unity of the divine life. Moreover, since the Son "is the logical presupposition and the actual condition for the procession of the Spirit from the Father," the procession "is connected with the generation relationally."[24]

Thus we have the formula: the Spirit proceeds from the Father of the Son. But, if with the Greeks there is "no ontological order whatsoever"[25] within the divine life, which Moltmann agrees with along with the Father's unique role in constituting (causing) the trinitarian reality, is it possible to think that the Spirit logically precedes the generation of the Son rather than merely "accompanying," "resting on," and "shining" in relation to the Son? Surely, Moltmann affirms an active role for the Spirit in the inner-trinitarian relations.[26] But how is this to be interpreted precisely *for the generation of the Son*? How strictly must we retain the traditional *taxis* (order of Father-Son-Spirit in the immanent Trinity)? This is the position of David Coffey to which we now turn.

2. David Coffey: A "Return" Model

"Coffey is among those Catholic theologians who attempt sympathetically to listen to the Orthodox East."[27] He describes his work as "a modern reconciling Spirit Christology"[28] that, as already cited in the introduction, moves from the data of the New Testament (apprehension), to the immanent Trinity (understanding), to the economic Trinity (judgment) as a validation of the biblical data. To do justice to the total data such a Spirit Christology (ascending based on the Synoptics) must incorporate a Logos Christology (descending based on John). It must also incorporate the correct insights of both East (the absolute priority of the Father) and West (the role of the Son in the procession of the Spirit). At the end of his book, *Deus Trinitas*, he proposes a simple formula that includes the concerns of both sides without explicitly stating the extreme position of either monopatrism or filioquism:

> Such, I suggest, is "The Holy Spirit proceeds from the Father and receives from the Son", which is well attested in Scripture and tradition. My argument in this book is that the mutual love theory best accommodates the various true, though at times apparently contradictory statements of both sides, and alone explains exactly what it is that the Holy Spirit receives from the Son, namely, the quality of being the Son's love of the Father, which, completing that of the Father for the Son, constitutes in its objectivization the person of the Holy Spirit.[29]

Hence, the Holy Spirit cannot be considered a person really and objectively without the mutual love of the Father and the Son.

Coffey proceeds methodologically by distinguishing a "procession model" from a "return model." Both are true but the return model is more comprehensive and so completes the procession model. With regard to the latter, the *taxis* is sacrosanct in both East and West and so cannot be changed for doctrinal reasons. This holds for the immanent Trinity in terms of the Father as cause of the hypostatic distinctions and the Son's involvement (*filioque* or *per filium*) in the hypostatic distinction of the Holy Spirit. This also holds true for the economic Trinity in the distinct missions: the Father sends the Son and the Son sends the Spirit. In the economic Trinity, however, there are *two taxeis*: Father-Son-Spirit (procession/mission) and Spirit-Son-Father (return). The return model is Coffey's original contribution. Here he locates the concern for a more active role of the Holy Spirit, that is, for a proper mission of the Holy Spirit in the salvific process. For us, the order of return has always been understood as a simple inversion of the order of procession, but this must be nuanced in terms of our relationship to Christ. Christ's relationship to the Holy Spirit, based on the ascending Christology of the Synoptics (and not on the traditional descending Christology of John) is unique: Father-Spirit-Son. Thus, Coffey emphasizes that from the moment of Jesus' conception the Holy Spirit is active and continues to be so throughout the mission of Jesus until its culmination in his death and resurrection when he returns the Spirit to the Father in love and communicates that same Spirit to us in that same love.

The ultimate goal of his work is to give a feasible account of the economic Trinity that presupposes but does not stop at either the biblical Trinity (which is the indispensable starting point) or the immanent Trinity (which, left at the level of understanding alone, would remain disconnected from the concrete history of salvation).[30] He argues that the biblical data in both John and the Synoptics is functional in character, whereas concerns about a metaphysical or ontological incarnation, which remain at the level of abstraction and are formed by the intellectual culture in which they arise, surface at the level of understanding. To arrive at the level of judgment (the economic Trinity), however, both the biblical and doctrinal developments are presupposed so that we cannot legitimately move back to an earlier oral and/or preconciliar stage. We are heirs of the written witnesses of both Scripture and creed. Moreover, a balanced theology will employ the procession model and the return model for a full and adequate use of the biblical evidence. This has ecumenical importance. "Because in the immanent Trinity the procession model deals with the unfolding of unity into diversity, it is the one more congenial to Western preoccupations. Conversely, because the return model, as model of union, had to do with the relations of the three divine persons among themselves, it corresponds better to Eastern emphases, even if in fact it is hardly accepted or even known in the East."[31]

In moving to the immanent Trinity from the biblical data, he aligns "the mission model" with "the procession or distinction model" and "the return model" with "the return or union model." That is to say, the mission of the Son as totally dependent on the Father who sends him and the mission of the Spirit, whom Jesus received in his conception and baptism and who is sent from the Father through the active mediation of the crucified and risen Christ, and therefore is dependent on both the Father and the Son for his mission to the Church, gives rise to the traditional *taxis* of Father-Son-Spirit (with the question of *per filium* and/or *filioque* still to be resolved). "Thus is provided the functional point of departure from which the ontological doctrine of the immanent Trinity (at least in one basic form) is extrapolated in the first four centuries of the Church."[32] The procession model aligned with the mission model deals with the outward movement of God to the world, the divine self-communication or self-revelation as triune. Here unity (the God of the Old Testament) unfolds into diversity. For the East that unity is not an abstract essence but the concrete reality of the Father who is the cause (*aitia*) of the Son and the Spirit. As noted in the previous chapter, the Father is the one who constitutes the hypostatic distinctions of Son and Spirit. Yet, as Coffey argues, the biblical data of both Father and Son as source of the Spirit's mission must be reflected in the inner-trinitarian life. The strength of the West (Augustine) has been to emphasize the unity of the divine life and hence the inseparability of the mediation of the Son in the hypostatic identity of the Spirit. This relationship of the Spirit to Father and Son can be clarified by the return model.

If the procession model is concerned with the outward self-communication of the triune life of God, the return model is concerned with our participation in the inner trinitarian life of God as the inverted order of Spirit-Son-Father. This is necessary to complement and complete the procession model. "Christ came forth from the Father only to return to him with us, in the Spirit of the Father."[33] In the case of Jesus as distinct from ourselves, however, the Spirit as the Father's creative and empowering love constitutes Jesus as the incarnate Son, accompanies him throughout his life of obedient love, and is the answering love of Jesus whom he returns to the Father. So now the order as complete is: Father-Spirit-Son-Spirit-Father. The Spirit is the bond of love between Father and Son, moving from God's power in creation to presence in inspiration to the supreme *personal* expression of the gift of love.[34] Jesus freely and radically appropriates the Spirit (the Father's love) as his own and on the cross returns that love to the Father and inseparably communicates it to us. In sum:

> ...the Father bestows the Holy Spirit on Jesus as his love for
> him in a uniquely radical way in which Jesus is brought into
> human existence as his beloved Son. Jesus further appro-
> priates this unique Gift of the Spirit and the divine Sonship
> which it brings about, in the course of his life through his
> unfailing obedience and answering love of the Father, and
> in his death definitively returns to the Father in love by

returning the Holy Spirit to him (though not thereby losing it himself). From this truly biblical theology the Holy Spirit emerges as the mutual love of the Father and Jesus Christ, his Son, even though, as Augustine pointed out, nowhere does Scripture actually call the Spirit love.[35]

Coffey emphasizes Jesus' answering love of the Father as the "missing link" between the Father's love of the Son and the Son's love of the Church and so indicates a proper mission of the Holy Spirit from the very inception of Jesus' life.[36] But he recognizes an apparent contradiction between the logical order of the traditional *taxis* in the procession model (which he maintains *must* be affirmed according to the official doctrinal tradition) and the differing *taxis* in the return model. In the immanent Trinity the Son proceeds from the Father without the Holy Spirit and then the Father bestows the Holy Spirit (his love) on the Son and the Son returns that love to the Father:

> According, then, to the traditional *taxis, first* there is the generation of the Son by the Father, and *second* there is the coincident bestowal of the Holy Spirit by the Father on the Son and the bestowal of the same Spirit by the Son on the Father. It is only as the *mutual* love of the Father and the Son, or rather as its objectivization, that the Holy Spirit has his existence. As mutual, the double bestowal of love, that is, by the Father and the Son on each other, must be coincident and indeed must constitute a single bestowal and a single act....But the Father's love for the Son always has priority over the Son's love for the Father, and the latter is always an answering love.[37]

Coffey makes "a distinction between 'two stages' of the Trinity, *in fieri* (in the process of becoming) and *in facto esse* (as already constituted)."[38] While the Trinity only exists as eternally constituted, the distinction is useful to try to understand the process of constituting the intratrinitarian distinctions. Thus, the Father has a "prevenient love," the Father's self-love whereby he generates the Son as in the procession model. But this must be complemented and completed in the return model of mutual love. There is a priority of the Father's love for the Son but this is reciprocated by the Son's love for the Father and in this

79

mutuality the Holy Spirit is constituted. Embracing both models, he can say that in the procession model the Holy Spirit is constituted by passive spiration but in the more comprehensive return model the Holy Spirit is constituted as the dynamic bond of active mediation between Father and Son.[39]

According to this proposal, the mutual love theory can accommodate the concerns of the East (the monarchy of the Father) and of the West (the consubstantiality of the three persons) because it represents a higher viewpoint. The logical order of the two models perceives the procession model as the foundation and prerequisite of the return model whereas the return model embraces the procession model as more comprehensive. "Put simply, the Filioque, which emerges from the procession model, *is* the mutual love theory of the return model....A truly balanced statement...would be, first, the Holy Spirit proceeds from the Father and the Son as from a single principle; and second, by way of clarification of this, the Holy Spirit proceeds from the Father and receives from the Son."[40] Whether such a formulation will be embraced is still a matter of ecumenical dialogue. Nonetheless, with his mutual love theory Coffey offers an alternative to Moltmann's proposal that the Spirit receives from the Father his divine *existence* and from the Son his relational *form*, the latter allowing the *filioque* to have its own proper place.[41]

Unlike the essentialism of the procession model, the return model is personal: the mutual love of two who love with one act of loving. The Father generates the Son as his image or likeness that gives rise to their love. Jesus' love for the Father and the Father's love for Jesus are clear and foundational in the Synoptics: "It was the contribution of the Synoptics to point out that this relationship was created, sustained, and fostered by the Holy Spirit of God bestowed by the Father in all fullness on Jesus at his conception. The reality of Jesus as presented in the gospels, then, is trinitarian, and its most basic feature is the mutual love existing in the Spirit between the Father and the Son."[42] The biblical data transposed into an understanding of the immanent Trinity as mutual love justifies the affirmation (judgment) that the Father (not God in the abstract) *personally* communicates himself to the Son (not the Logos) in the incarnation and that the Spirit as Christ's *human*[43] love of both the Father and ourselves is received in the Church as the personal self-communication of the Father and the Son that we call grace. The Father, then, is the

"Giver," the Son is the "Receiver," and the Spirit is the "Gift" as both given and received.[44]

In conclusion, and as a transition to the view of Thomas Weinandy, both Moltmann and Coffey seek to address the concerns of Eastern Orthodoxy in ways that could be compatible with the West. Both affirm the absolute priority of the Father as cause or origin of the trinitarian persons. Both seek ways to understand the relationship of the Son and the Spirit in the immanent Trinity that have their foundation in the biblical data. Coffey's move from the procession model to the return model enables him to affirm the traditional *taxis* that necessitates the Son's involvement in the procession of the Spirit, that is, the Spirit "receives" from the Son the Son's love of the Father that constitutes the Spirit not only as the passive recipient of spiration but at the same time in view of the return model as the active dynamism of the mutual love of the Father and the Son. The Spirit's proper role is the bond or union of love between Father and Son. Moltmann, on the other hand, affirms on the basis of God's essential nature as love that each of the persons is love in a distinctive way. The Father and Son love each other, so that the Spirit's proper role is not love but the manifestation of the glory and beauty of the triune life in the unity of ecstatic bliss. Whereas for Coffey the Spirit is constituted as person by the mutual love, for Moltmann the Spirit is constituted as person by the Father who equally generates the Son and breathes forth the Spirit. Unlike Coffey, the Father has two names: "Father" in relation to the Son and "Producer" in relation to the Spirit. Likewise, the Spirit in relation to the Father is the Father's "Spirit" (or breath, related to the Son as "Word") and in relation to the Son "Light." In this connection, Moltmann denies the *filioque* because each person in relation to the other is unique and has a distinctive role. The Spirit is already constituted and active as person because of his relation to the Father *alone*. What the Spirit receives from the Son is not personal existence but relational form (in this sense, as differentiated, he can admit a place for the *filioque*). Moltmann sees dangers in both an undifferentiated *filioque* and in an undifferentiated monarchy of the Father because they rely on general concepts rather than on "concrete differences." The Father, the Son, and the Holy Spirit

> ...differ not only in their mutual relations, but also in respect of their personhood, even if the person is to be

81

grasped in its relations and not apart from them. If one wishes to remain concrete, one must apply a different concept of "person" respectively to the Father, the Son and the Spirit. Their designation as divine persons already contains within itself a tendency to modalism. The general categories of *hypostasis* or person bring to the fore the common and similar in them, not the particular and distinct.[45]

While both authors are concerned with mutual reciprocity in the inner divine life, they differ on how the Spirit as person is constituted, i.e., on what the Spirit receives from the Son.[46] Neither author thinks that we can argue from the economic Trinity to the immanent Trinity (though the biblical data of salvation in history is foundational and indispensable). Moltmann appeals to the trinitarian doxology that goes beyond the economic Trinity of salvation history and eucharistic worship in order to attain the true apprehension of the immanent Trinity. This is to arrive at the community of perfect love in a social understanding of perichoretic unity. Coffey, on the other hand, appeals to two models that must balance each other. The procession model maintains the traditional *taxis* and so the necessity of the *filioque*. The return model, which entails the different *taxis* of Father, Spirit, Son, assumes that the Father bestows the Spirit on the Son and the Son who makes the Spirit his own returns the Spirit to the Father through the whole historical and salvific process of conception, ministry, death, and resurrection. This leads to an understanding of the immanent Trinity as mutual love.

As we move to a consideration of Thomas Weinandy, there is a curious difference between Coffey and Weinandy on the interpretation of Luke 1:35 that should be noted at the outset. Coffey interprets the text in its given sequence of creation ("the child to be born"), sanctification ("will be holy"), incarnation ("Son of God"). Thus, the Holy Spirit is accorded an active role from the very beginning of the mission of the Son as creating the humanity, sanctifying it and disposing it for union with the Son. Although Coffey denies it on the basis of his two models, should not his methodological principle that the immanent Trinity must be derived from the biblical data and not from philosophical and cosmological speculation apply here? Yet, while Coffey's view of Luke 1:35 might support Weinandy's view of the active priority of the Spirit in the generation of the Son, Weinandy rejects it on the grounds that the Holy Spirit cannot sanctify the humanity prior to the union.[47] Before engaging that question, we must first review the approach of Thomas Weinandy.

3. Thomas Weinandy: An "Interactive" Model

Along with Moltmann and Coffey, perhaps even more intentionally so, Weinandy sees his proposal of reciprocal interaction of all three persons as having "ecumenical significance," especially in addressing the controversy over the *filioque*. He devotes chapter 5, "The Ecumenical Significance of the Thesis" (87–100), to this issue and declares "an ecumenical convergence" that safeguards and transcends the concerns of both East and West.

> By giving the Holy Spirit his proper role within the Trinity the controversy over the procession is surmounted for the entire conception of the Trinity is now transfigured and redesigned. Not only does the Holy Spirit proceed principally from the Father (the concern of the East) and derivatively from the Son (the concern of the West), but the Spirit in proceeding from the Father as the one in whom the Son is begotten now actively conforms the Father to be Father for the Son and conforms the Son to be Son for the Father. It is this active role of the Spirit, by which he himself is defined in relation to the Father and the Son, which neither the East nor the West has appreciated. Yet it is precisely this active role of the Spirit which safeguards their concerns and even transcends them.[48]

He affirms the Spirit's active role as singular and proper and so understands the Trinity in a more symmetrical and harmonious way. The integration of the active role of the Holy Spirit equally with the Father and the Son, a "perichoresis of action" that constitutes each person in their distinctiveness, is the key:

> While the Son and the Holy Spirit come forth from the Father, yet in the coming forth all three persons become who they are, and they do so precisely in reciprocally inter-

acting upon one another, simultaneously fashioning one another to be who they are and so becoming who they are in themselves. None of the persons is purely passive; not even the Holy Spirit.[49]

In his preface, he states clearly what he is setting out to do: "This book has one simple objective. I want to argue that within the Trinity the Father begets the Son in or by the Holy Spirit, who proceeds then from the Father as the one in whom the Son is begotten."[50]

In the introduction, he argues for the inadequacies of the traditional views of both East and West, grounded as they are in the philosophical notions of Platonic emanationism (East) and of Aristotelian epistemology (West) so that the Father's priority leads to a kind of sequentialism of precedence and subordination. Thus, in the East the Cappadocian emphasis on the Father alone as the underived deity can lead to the Son and the Spirit as derived and implicitly subordinate, while in the West the Augustinian emphasis on knowledge as preceding love can lead to the passivity and subordination of the Spirit. Weinandy affirms the biblical imperative that the Son and the Spirit depend upon the Father, but he will argue that there is "an order of origin and derivation" but not "an order of priority, precedence, and sequence." "A proper understanding of the Trinity can only be obtained if all three persons, logically and ontologically, spring forth in one simultaneous, nonsequential, eternal act in which each person of the Trinity subsistently defines, and equally is subsistently defined by, the other persons."[51]

Methodologically, the design of his argument, not unlike Coffey, moves from the biblical data (what he calls a "functional economic trinitarianism" but note that Coffey reserves the economic Trinity to the level of judgment) to the immanent Trinity as he reconceives it ontologically. He divides the biblical data into the early proclamation (kerygma), which includes Jesus' baptism, death, and resurrection, and the later proclamation, which includes the infancy narratives and the Johannine literature. We have given our own version of this in chapter 2, but his analysis of the biblical data in support of his thesis does provide a convincing basis, especially for the active role of Father, Son, and Spirit in the economy of salvation. For our purposes, it is his systematic understanding of the immanent Trinity as based on the biblical evidence that will be the focus.

In chapter 4, "A New Trinitarian Ontology" (53–85), he treats "the origin and action" of the Father, then the Son, then the Spirit. "What is the precise nature of the Father's paternity? In the conflicting answers to this question lies the real origin of the estrangement between the East and the West."[52] The customary distinction made that the West begins with the unity of God and the East with the three persons needs qualification. For both East and West God's essence is inseparably the interrelationship of the persons. The distinction of essence and person in God does not exist in reality but only in "our way of thinking."[53] In sum:

> The Godhead is neither in the Father alone nor is it a solitary substance distinct from the Trinity. The Godhead is the Trinity. The one Godhead, the one being of God, is the action of the Father begetting the Son and spirating the Spirit, and so sharing with them the whole of his deity, constituting them as equal divine persons. Thus the monarchy of the Father is maintained, but within the one being of God who is a trinity of persons.[54]

The Father communicates the whole of himself to the Son except his fatherhood. Weinandy applauds the efforts of John Zizioulas and Colin Gunton to maintain that the appropriate ontological category to understand the Godhead is person (*hypostasis*) and not substance, but this must be understood as inherently dynamic and as applicable not only to the Father as the dynamic source of the Son and the Spirit but also to the Son and Spirit as being in a dynamic relationship to the Father. This latter emphasis is what has been lacking. "What one needs to grasp is that the whole oneness of God's being (the *homoousios*) is itself a trinity of persons."[55]

In turning to the Son, he emphasizes the passive character of the Son as begotten and asks the question: "Is there a reciprocal act that the Son performs which equally constitutes his being the Son in relationship to the Father and so, in some sense, constitutes the Father as Father? This question can only be answered in light of the role of the Holy Spirit."[56]

"The question never fully addressed by either tradition is this: if both the Son and the Spirit proceed from the Father, what is there in the nature of the Father's fatherhood that gives rise to the Spirit without making the Spirit another son?"[57] The answer is to recognize the active role of the Spirit in the begetting of the Son. "The Father spirates the Spirit in the same act by which he begets the Son, for the Spirit proceeds from the Father as the fatherly Love in whom or by whom the Son is begotten."[58] The Spirit then is the love in whom the Son is begotten. Unlike the Aristotelian view adopted in the West, Weinandy sees knowing and loving as simultaneous in the Trinity. "The Father does not, even logically, first beget the Son and then love the Son in the Spirit. The begetting of the Son and the proceeding of the Spirit are simultaneous and, while distinct, mutually inhere in one another."[59] Thus, the fatherly love of the Father and the filial love of the Son are the action of the Spirit. The "perichoresis of action" constitutes each of the persons as active in their relation to the others.

In conclusion, Weinandy's proposal advocates the "interactive" role of each of the persons who subsist in a distinctive way as person in relation to the others. While he frequently refers to Moltmann and Coffey as close to his own view, there are significant differences. With Moltmann, he affirms the original perichoretic triunity and the resultant critique of the monarchy of the Father as the one who *alone* constitutes the other persons, but he also affirms the ineluctable unity of the divine nature (monotheism) and develops more clearly the *active* role of the Holy Spirit as the person who subsists as the source of the complementarity of the Father and Son:

> Because each of the persons now actively plays a role in determining the subjectivity of the others, they complement one another. The Father is Father not only in opposition to the Son and the Son is Son not only in opposition to the Father, but they also, in their relatedness, complement one another as being, respectively, Father for the Son and Son for the Father. This complementarity of the persons as subsistent relations is due again to the Holy Spirit....The Trinity of persons then subsists in opposition to one another only as complementary relations.[60]

With Coffey, he affirms the Holy Spirit as the mutual love between the Father and the Son, but he revises the traditional *taxis* within the immanent Trinity in a way that Coffey rejects.[61] Coffey argues that the procession-mission model of Father-Son-Spirit is based in the biblical data and is sacrosanct because of doctrinal development. Hence, he proposes an alternative model with a different *taxis* of Father-Spirit-Son also based in the biblical data of an ascending Christology and a necessary complement to and completion of the traditional model. The traditional *taxis* reflects "the order of origination" but is this the only activity that can be attributed to divine persons? Coffey thinks so: "Unless we are talking about 'essential' acts, i.e., acts common to all three persons because performed in the first instance by the divine essence or God as such, the only acts a divine person can perform in regard to another are 'notional' acts, i.e., originating acts."[62] Weinandy's interactive model, on the other hand, allows for complementarity that can include simultaneously the ascending and descending models. If the Holy Spirit is the Father's love for the Son at the moment of Jesus' conception, following Coffey's analysis of Luke 1:35 that the Spirit creates, sanctifies, and so disposes the humanity for the Son who unites himself to this particular humanity, and if the Son's love for the Father is a process of appropriation until the Son returns that love to the Father, why can this trinitarian pattern of mutual love not be said of the immanent Trinity in its originating acts?

In my view, Weinandy overcomes the inadequacy of the procession model as isolating the Father's love of the Son as self-love (recognized by Coffey) and moves the model of mutual love to the center of trinitarian thinking. It does this by affirming a more active role for the Holy Spirit in the inner-trinitarian life as well as in our own through the process of the history of salvation. Finally, Weinandy avers that while the tradition has not explicitly articulated his position, "it denies nothing that the councils have defined or the creeds proclaimed." Moreover, it advances the doctrinal understanding of the Trinity "in an orthodox manner [so] that the *filioque* debate is transcended and surmounted."[63] His hope is that Eastern and Western theologians alike will scrutinize his proposal to advance the cause of Christian unity.

Conclusion

THE POWER THAT SETS US FREE

This book has not intended to produce a complete and adequate treatment of the doctrine of the Trinity. Rather, it is an essay in trinitarian Christology that addresses two major concerns. First, Christology must be *trinitarian* insofar as it addresses and advocates a more active role of the Holy Spirit as a person, a role that is both singular and proper. This includes both the economic activity of the triune life in creation and the dynamic, perichoretic interactive life of God as God, that is, within the inner and eternal divine life. Second, Christology must be *ecumenical* insofar as it addresses the concerns of both East and West with regard to the *filioque*. While it is important ecumenically to return to the original creed of 381, the theological issues that have developed over the centuries cannot be avoided or circumvented. The question finally is whether East and West can come to a convergence of views.

Clearly, there are differences of opinion among Eastern theologians themselves and equally among Western theologians. This book has presented a partial sampling, admittedly with a view to finding representative Western theologians who seek in creative ways to develop insights that are potentially compatible with the East. The views of Moltmann, Coffey, and Weinandy differ, yet each affirms the possibility of a higher viewpoint that would either qualify the *filioque* or eliminate it. All three authors seek a way of affirming the complementarity of the three divine persons within the divine life. Moltmann emphasizes the inseparable identity of the immanent and economic Trinity and accepts the *filioque* only in the differentiated sense that the Spirit who is constituted in existence as person by the Father alone

88

receives from the Son the relational form of Light and so constitutes the "bliss" of the divine life. Coffey focuses on the Spirit's active role in Jesus' historical life. Thus, he distinguishes the procession model, which, according to the tradition of *taxis*, necessitates the *filioque*, from the return model, which complements and completes the former by affirming that Jesus returns the Spirit to the Father so that the Spirit becomes the fully constituted bond of love between the Father and the Son. Weinandy proposes the Spirit's active role in the eternal begetting of the Son, a "perichoresis of action" that constitutes each person in their distinctiveness. Thus, all three persons are active in constituting the triune life. In the eternal simultaneity each person subsistently defines and is defined by the other persons. As with the Eastern view, the trinity of persons is the given reality that is the oneness of God's being. In a word, the Spirit is active in the complementarity of the persons. Weinandy's view is attractive insofar as it transcends the necessity of the *filioque* altogether. Such a view would, I hope, engage a response from Eastern theologians in the interests of ecumenical unity.

Finally, however, the importance of the Trinity is not primarily a matter of doctrine as precise concepts but, as Walter Kasper observes, a matter of the grammar of doxology. Both East and West can agree that all theology is *practical* in the sense that it is oriented to the fullness of human life, so that we will be fully alive and free as God has intended us to be. This is the "mystical theology of the Eastern Church," as Lossky proposes, but it must embrace not only the vertical height and depth of mystical praxis but also the horizontal length of emancipatory praxis as well as the comprehensive breadth of the cosmic and all-embracing breath that we call the Holy Spirit. The fullness of God is the power that sets us free. As Paul said so well: "For freedom Christ has set us free" (Gal 5:1). And further: "If we live by the Spirit, let us also be guided by the Spirit" (Gal 5:25). Indeed, the Spirit will lead us into all truth and that means into the very life of God.

Notes

Introduction

1. Author's translation and italics. Unless otherwise noted, in this chapter biblical translations are the author's own.

2. Rudolf Schnackenburg *Ephesians: A Commentary*, trans. Helen Heron (Edinburgh: T&T Clark, 1991), commenting on 3:19, observes that Christians "...are led more and more to God the Father in Christ through the Holy Spirit. Here we observe a certain trinitarian structure (as in the Great Eulogy 1.3–14). Admittedly it is not a theological reflection about the trinitarian God but a consideration of the Economy of Salvation in which the reality of God is opened up in its effect on us" (152).

3. The verb used, *anakephalaiosasthai*, "...chiefly means 'to summarize, sum up'. In the context of the passage here it is not the temporal aspect (assumption and summation of earlier things) which is dominant but the spatial aspect, the relation and integration of (till now) separated spheres. 'Things in heaven and things on earth' will (again) be united into one whole" Ibid., 60.

4. Jürgen Moltmann, "The Trinitarian Personhood of the Holy Spirit" in Bradford E. Hinze and D. Lyle Dabney, eds., *Advents of the Spirit: An Introduction to the Current Study of Pneumatology* (Milwaukee: Marquette University Press, 2001), 303. His article, based on a more developed treatment in his *The Spirit of Life: A Universal Affirmation*, trans. Margaret Kohl (Minneapolis: Fortress Press, 1992), 289–306, treats successively the monarchical, eschatological, eucharistic, and doxological Trinity. Only the last of these moves beyond the economic Trinity to the immanent Trinity, the Holy Spirit who with the Father and the Son is worshipped and glorified, according to the Creed of Constantinople I of 381. Moltmann calls this a "social" understanding of the Trinity in perichoretic equality and unity.

5.   In Ephesians 1—3 the author makes a strong identification of God's fullness with the Church as the body of Christ (especially at 1:22–23; see as well 2:10, 18; 3:10, 19, 21; 4:13, 15, 24; 5:32) and yet has a longer and equally strong section (chaps. 4–6) exhorting the members of the Church to overcome struggles and divisions and to live faithfully in the love of Christ. Schnackenburg commenting on 1:10 (*Ephesians*, 61) and on 1:23 (ibid., 83–84) notes that Christ already rules and as ruler penetrates every part of the universe. The Church is the beneficent sphere of his rule and yet still struggles in a cosmic battle for the final redemption which is still to come.

6.   Schnackenburg, *Ephesians*, 151–152. The "strengthening" of v. 18 (*eksischysete* only here in the NT) "…is interpreted to mean especially that they should be increasingly able to comprehend with all the faithful the scope of the divine plan for salvation and the love of Christ which surpasses knowledge in order to be drawn in to the total fullness of the divine riches" Ibid., 153.

7.   Bernd Jochen Hilberath, "Identity Through Self-Transcendence: The Holy Spirit and the Fellowship of Free Persons" in Hinze and Dabney, *Advents*, 268.

8.   Ibid., 291. The image of "breadth" or "making room" for another to live within oneself has a particular resonance with female experience. Hilberath refers to the work of H. Schuengel-Straumann in ibid., 269, 292. See also Elizabeth A. Johnson, *She Who Is: The Mystery of God in Feminist Theological Discourse* (New York: Crossroad, 1992), 234: "…to be so structured that you have room inside yourself for another to dwell is quintessentially a female experience. To have another actually living and moving and having being in yourself is likewise the province of women. So too is the experience of contraction as a condition for bringing others to life in their own integrity."

9.   Schnackenburg, *Ephesians*, 152–153, 305–308.

10.   These observations are inspired by the reflections of Wolfhart Pannenberg, *Systematic Theology*, vol. 1, trans. Geoffrey W. Bromiley (Grand Rapids, MI: Eerdmans, 1991), 300–336, especially 330–333: "Viewing the immanent Trinity and the economic Trinity as one presupposes the development of a concept of God which can grasp in one not only the transcendence of the divine being and his immanence in the world but also the eternal self-identity of God and the debatability of his truth in the process of

history, along with the decision made concerning it by the consummation of history" (333).

11.   The confusion that arises from different uses of the word *immanent* is one of Catherine LaCugna's objections to the term in *God for Us: The Trinity and Christian Life* (New York: Harper San Francisco, 1991), 224–230.

12.   Roger Haight, *Jesus Symbol of God* (Maryknoll, NY: Orbis, 1999).

13.   The Vatican Congregation for the Doctrine of the Faith published a notification on the book in the English edition of *L'Osservatore Romano* on February 9, 2005, declaring that the book "contains serious doctrinal errors regarding certain fundamental truths of faith." While I am in agreement with the substance of the Congregation's concerns, especially regarding the divinity of Jesus and the consequences for the Trinity, I find that a number of their statements imply a fundamentalist reading of Scripture that simply ignores and certainly fails to engage contemporary biblical studies. Haight's attempt to engage the contemporary world and especially the pervasive sense of historical consciousness seems lost on the Congregation. I am also in agreement with the ensuing statement of the board of directors of the Catholic Theological Society of America to the effect that Roger Haight has welcomed critique of his work and dialogue about its contents and significance, that this has been ongoing among professional theologians in various journals and at the meetings of the CTSA itself, and that the prohibition from teaching Catholic theology impugns his personal integrity and responsibility and undermines his standing among his professional peers, which is considerable.

14.   Prior to publication of the book in 1999, there has been a history of discussion of Haight's proposals, notably: Roger Haight, SJ, "The Case for Spirit Christology," *Theological Studies* 53 (1992): 257–287; John H. Wright, SJ, "Roger Haight's Spirit Christology," *Theological Studies* 53 (1992): 729–735; and the report of Michael Slusser on the "Seminar on Christology" in CTSA *Proceedings of the Forty-Eighth Annual Convention* (1993): 143–145. Wright makes the decisive point that while one can accept both a Spirit Christology and a Word Christology properly understood, the central confession of faith is "that Jesus Christ is the eternal Son of God made human…" (735). Indeed, the primary biblical image of Jesus is not Logos or Spirit

but Son and the language of Spirit and Word function in relation to this foundational link.

15. These views are developed in my essay, "Revelation as Metaphoric Process," *Theological Studies* 47 (1986): 388–411. The proposal of another category, i.e., constitutive but not normative, is found at 410–411 and especially n. 69.

16. Haight refers to my book *Christology as Narrative Quest* (Collegeville, MN: Liturgical Press, 1997), 11, nn. 13 and 15, but he does not engage my affirmation: "...a balanced view affirms the importance and necessity of both metaphorical and literal speech. Rather than play one off against the other in either-or fashion, we must analyze the propriety and necessity of each in given speech situations" (37). Two examples of literal speech about God that I suggest are that God is *real* and that God is *active*.

17. This is the whole point of my book *Christology as Narrative Quest*. On the inadequacy of both the Alexandrian and the Antiochene views, see 120–129.

18. To remain true to both the tradition and the Gospel narratives, one must say both that the divine Word constitutes Jesus concretely and uniquely in his human (hypostatic) existence and that the human subjectivity of the Word is the full, free human knowledge and will of Jesus in his earthly life and in his transformed existence as risen.

19. Ralph Del Colle, *Christ and the Spirit: Spirit-Christology in Trinitarian Perspective* (New York: Oxford University Press, 1994), 3.

20. David Coffey, "Spirit Christology and the Trinity" in Hinze and Dabney, *Advents*, 315, 318.

21. Ibid., 323.

22. Ibid., 323–324 (italics in original).

23. David Coffey, *Deus Trinitas: The Doctrine of the Triune God* (New York: Oxford University Press, 1999), 16, 17 (italics in original).

24. Pannenberg, *Systematic Theology*, vol. 1, 394.

25. Walter Kasper, *The God of Jesus Christ*, trans. Matthew J. O'Connell (New York: Crossroad, 1986), 276 (italics added). Pannenberg agrees with Kasper that we cannot simply absorb the immanent Trinity in the economic Trinity since the Trinity is the same in salvation history as in eternity, but he thinks in disagreement with Kasper that we can argue from the economic Trinity to the immanent Trinity. Pannenberg, *Systematic Theology*, vol. 1, 330–331 and n. 213. Kasper

and Coffey both see the sequence of the argument differently from Pannenberg.

26. Bernard Cooke, *Power and the Spirit of God: Toward an Experience-Based Pneumatology* (New York: Oxford University Press, 2004), offers a phenomenological analysis of the diverse human experiences of power and connects each to theological reflections on the Spirit. His "unifying metaphor" is "the *experience of a personal embrace*" (183, italics in original) that resonates with Jesus in the bosom of the Father (John 1:18) and, I would add, with the Beloved Disciple in the bosom of Jesus (John 13:23).

Chapter One

1. The need to address poverty, culture, and interreligious dialogue for effective evangelization in the contemporary world has been emphasized by the Asian Bishops. See the abundant references in Thomas C. Fox, *Pentecost in Asia: A New Way of Being Church* (Maryknoll, NY: Orbis, 2002). See also the many works of Peter C. Phan, for example his *Being Religious Interreligiously: Asian Perspectives on Interreligious Dialogue* (Maryknoll, NY: Orbis, 2004).

2. Howard J. Van Till, "The Creation: Intelligently Designed or Optimally Equipped?" *Theology Today* 55 (1998): 364 (italics in original). The whole issue is on theology and science.

3. Diarmuid O'Murchú, *Quantum Theology: Spiritual Implications of the New Physics* (New York: Crossroad, 1997), 205–206, from appendix 2, "Doing Theology in a Space-Time Continuum." He draws the conclusion that today "*cosmology* and not *theology* is the queen of the sciences" (206, italics in original). The issue is not about one replacing the other, however, but about whether each engages the other within the parameters of their own competence.

4. Neil Ormerod, "A Dialectic Engagement with the Social Sciences in an Ecclesiological Context," *Theological Studies* 66 (2005): 815-840.

5. C. G. Jung cited in O'Murchú, *Quantum Theology*, 137, introducing a chapter entitled "Integrating the Shadow." Cf. Sebastian Moore's concern to reconstruct the psychological processes of the disciples' experience of the paschal mystery as conversion "and the concomitant emergence of a trinitarian pattern in their God-consciousness" as analyzed by

Anne Hunt, *Trinity: Nexus of the Mysteries of Christian Faith* (Maryknoll, NY: Orbis, 2005), 84. Her review of Moore's position is on 79–85.

6.   Stephen W. Hawking, *A Brief History of Time* (New York: Bantam Books, 1988), 175; cited as the frontispiece by Paul Davies, *The Mind of God: The Scientific Basis for a Rational World* (New York: Simon & Schuster, 1992).

7.   Davies, *Mind*, 16.

8.   Ibid., 140–160 (chap. 6 is entitled "The Mathematical Secret").

9.   Ibid., 232.

10.   The strong anthropic principle holds that the universe is so designed as to produce human consciousness; the weak, that if the universe were even minutely different, we would not be here to observe it.

11.   Davies, *Mind*, 175. He refers to scientists who see the beauty of mathematical elegance as a guiding principle in theoretical physics more fundamental than experimental verification.

12.   Diarmuid O'Murchú, *Evolutionary Faith: Rediscovering God in Our Great Story* (Maryknoll, NY: Orbis, 2002), 9.

13.   Ibid., 12.

14.   Ibid., 51.

15.   Ibid., 54–55.

16.   Ibid., 176.

17.   Ibid., 179.

18.   Ibid., 179–181, 191–194. For an insightful treatment of the true mystic, see James W. Douglass, *Resistance and Contemplation* (New York: Dell, 1972).

19.   O'Murchú, *Evolutionary Faith*, 197–206.

20.   John F. Haught, *Deeper Than Darwin: The Prospect for Religion in the Age of Evolution* (Boulder, CO: Westview Press, 2003), xi-xvi. See *God After Darwin. A Theology of Evolution* (Boulder, CO: Westview Press, 2000), 45–56 (chap. 4 is entitled "Darwin's Gift to Theology"), where he proposes a theology of evolution rather than intelligent design theory. "Rather than attuning theology and human life to the restlessness and ambiguity of an unfinished universe, advocates of 'intelligent design' typically ignore the contingency, randomness, and struggle in evolution. But it is precisely the latter that a theology of evolution needs to take into account" (45).

21. Haught, *Deeper*, xiv.

22. Ibid., xv.

23. This is the central question of both the books in n. 20 as well as in "Darwin, Design and the Promise of Nature" (the Boyle lecture of February 4, 2004) and in *Responses to 101 Questions on God and Evolution* (New York/Mahwah, NJ: Paulist Press, 2001) 99–120 (qq. 69–86).

24. Haught, *Deeper*, 25 (italics in original).

25. Ibid., 154–159.

26. See the collection of essays in John Polkinghorne, ed., *The Work of Love: Creation as Kenosis* (Grand Rapids, MI: Eerdmans, 2001).

27. Walter Wink, *The Human Being: Jesus and the Enigma of the Son of the Man* (Minneapolis: Fortress Press, 2002), 1.

28. Ibid., 272, n. 1 and the "Glossary," 270–271.

29. Ibid., 32.

30. Ibid., Appendix 3. "Ezekiel's Influence on Jesus" (267–269). He draws a number of convincing parallels based on their roles as "son of man," e.g., both rejected and treated with contempt, both given judgment over the people, both bearing the people's iniquities. Other parallels deal mostly with images and modes of expression.

31. Ibid., 22.

32. Ibid., 259.

33. Ibid., 193 (italics in original).

34. Ibid., 256.

35. Ibid., 260.

36. See the articles by D. Lyle Dabney, "Why Should the Last Be First? The Priority of Pneumatology in Recent Theological Discussion," and by Bernd Jochen Hilberath, "Identity through Self-Transcendence: The Holy Spirit and the Fellowship of Free Persons" in Hinze and Dabney, *Advents*, 240–261 and 265–294. The cosmic significance of the Creator Spirit is one of the strengths of Denis Edwards, *Breath of Life: A Theology of the Creator Spirit* (Maryknoll, NY: Orbis, 2004). Kilian McDonnell shows how pervasive this forgetfulness has been, stretching back to Augustine's lament in 393 and earlier. See Kilian McDonnell, OSB, "A Trinitarian Theology of the Holy Spirit?" *Theological Studies* 46 (1985): 191–227, especially 191–193 and 194–200.

37. McDonnell, "A Trinitarian Theology," 203. He raises a number of exegetical questions posed by various commentators on Scripture.

38. In "A Response to Bernd Jochen Hilberath," Hinze and Dabney, *Advents*, 295–301, he emphatically concludes with the importance both methodologically and theologically of this contact function. See also, Kilian McDonnell, OSB, "Theological Presuppositions in Our Preaching about the Spirit," *Theological Studies* 59 (1998): 219–235.

39. McDonnell, "A Trinitarian Theology," 208.

40. Ibid., 210–212.

41. Ibid., 217.

42. Ibid., 226.

43. Elizabeth A. Dreyer, "An Advent of the Spirit: Medieval Mystics and Saints" in Hinze and Dabney, *Advents*, 123–162, explores a variety of images, including Bernard of Clairvaux's image of the Spirit as "kiss of the beloved." Bernard Cooke prefers the experience of "a personal embrace."

44. McDonnell, "A Trinitarian Theology," 226.

45. Theodore Stylianopoulos, "The Orthodox Position," in Hans Küng and Jürgen Moltmann, eds., *Conflicts About the Holy Spirit*: Concilium 128 (New York: Seabury Press, 1979), 23–30, comments on the different theological approaches of Augustine vis-à-vis Athanasius and the Cappodocians in terms of (1) style (personal theological speculation vs. a pastoral and practical concern); (2) historical context (Athanasius and the Cappodocians defending the faith against heretics in an ongoing debate whereas Augustine is removed from this context); (3) doctrinal value (only normative teaching is that of the ecumenical councils vs. Augustine's theological opinion).

46. For the questions on *taxis*, subordination, and the Spirit as the Spirit of Christ, see Dietrich Ritschl, "The History of the Filioque Controversy," in *Conflicts about the Holy Spirit*. Also see Ritschl's "Historical Development and Implications of the Filioque Controversy" in Lukas Vischer, ed., *Spirit of God, Spirit of Christ: Ecumenical Reflections on the Filioque Controversy*. WCC Faith & Order Paper 103 (London: SPCK, 1981), 46–65.

47. For an interesting and readable attempt to answer this question, see Ted Peters, *God as Trinity: Relationality and Temporality in Divine Life* (Louisville: Westminster/John Knox, 1993).

48. Such dialogues are found in Vischer's *Spirit of God, Spirit of Christ*, as well as in Paul R. Fries and Tiran Nersoyan, eds., *Christ in East and West* (Macon, GA: Mercer University Press, 1987). The second volume includes

discussions between the "Oriental Orthodox Churches" (Armenian, Ethiopian, Coptic, Indian, and Syrian) and the "Eastern Orthodox Churches" (Greek, Russian, Antiochian) as well as between Roman Catholic and Oriental Orthodox theologians (references to earlier publications of these dialogues are given on xiii). The volume also includes Protestant views of the dialogue (Lutheran, Southern Baptist, Mennonite, United Methodist, Disciples of Christ, and Presbyterian). For a clear presentation of the differences between Oriental and Eastern within the Orthodox Church, see Timothy Ware (Bishop Kallistos of Diokleia), *The Orthodox Church* (London: Penguin Books, 1997), 3–8.

49. Vladimir Lossky, *The Mystical Theology of the Eastern Church* (Cambridge and London: James Clarke & Co., 1957; trans. from French original of 1944), 13, 56.

50. Ibid., 42.

51. Ibid., 54–55.

52. Ibid., 73.

53. Ibid., 85–86.

54. Ibid., 92–93.

55. Ibid., 112–113.

56. Aloys Grillmeier, "The Understanding of the Christological Definitions of Both (Oriental Orthodox and Roman Catholic) Traditions in the Light of the Post-Chalcedonian Theology (Analysis of Terminologies in a Conceptual Framework)" in Fries and Nersoyan, *Christ in East and West*, 66–74.

57. Lossky, *Mystical*, 146.

58. John Meyendorff, *Christ in Eastern Christian Thought* (Washington, DC: Corpus Books, 1969), 158 (italics in original). The summary of Palamas's view in the text is derived from 156–161.

59. Ibid., 160.

60. Lossky, *Mystical*, 158–160.

61. Ibid., 166.

62. Ibid., 176 (italics in original). See also John D. Zizioulas, *Being as Communion. Studies in Personhood and the Church* (Crestwood, NY: St. Vladimir's Seminary Press, 1985), 49–65, who strongly emphasizes the ecclesiological significance of the person because the triune life is being as a communion of persons. "The being of God is a relational being: without the concept of communion it would not be possible to speak of the being of God....It would be unthinkable to speak of the 'one God' before

speaking of the God who is 'communion', that is to say, of the Holy Trinity. The Holy Trinity is a *primordial* ontological concept....The substance of God, 'God', has no ontological content, no true being, apart from communion," 17 (italics in original).

63. Lossky, *Mystical*, 213–214.

64. Ibid., 243.

65. Ibid., 246. On 240–245 he offers a clear summary of the main themes of the book.

66. Ibid., 237–238. André de Halleux, "Towards an Ecumenical Agreement on the Procession of the Holy Spirit and the Addition of the Filioque to the Creed" in Vischer, *Spirit of God, Spirit of Christ*, 69–84, proposes moving beyond polemics (e.g., Vladimir Lossky who accuses the West of being essentialist, rationalist, and authoritarian) to two complementary traditions rooted in each side's patristic traditions. In the same volume, Alasdair Heron, "The Filioque in Recent Reformed Theology," 110–117, summarizes Lossky's critique of Western theology as having four tendencies: (1) a monistic and/or unitarian tendency with regard to the Trinity; (2) a tendency to subordinate the Holy Spirit with regard to Christology; (3) a tendency to narrow the focus upon the cross with regard to soteriology; and (4) a tendency to ignore the freedom of the Holy Spirit with an ecclesial or biblical authoritarianism with regard to ecclesiology.

67. Meyendorff, *Christ*, 166.

68. Ibid.

Chapter Two

1. Bernard Lonergan, "Mission and the Spirit" in Peter Huizing and William Bassett, eds., *Experience of the Spirit*. Concilium vol. 9, no. 10 (New York: The Seabury Press, 1974), 77.

2. Anne Hunt, "Psychological Analogy and Paschal Mystery in Trinitarian Theology," *Theological Studies* 59 (1998): 197–218, especially her analysis of Hans Urs von Balthasar's focus on the "aesthetic act" of faith vis-à-vis Bernard Lonergan's intentionality analysis. Both converge in their emphasis on "the dynamic state of being in love" (209, quoting Lonergan). But von Balthasar's attempt to articulate the mystery of the Trinity in the context of the paschal mystery (as known in revelation) does challenge metaphysical assumptions about divine

immutability and impassibility. Hunt concludes: "Balthasar's trinitarian theology is a notable example of the divine mystery exploding into our theologizing and blowing open our most heroic attempts to conceptualize and systematize" (218). See also Anne Hunt, *What Are They Saying About the Trinity?* (New York/Mahwah, NJ: Paulist Press, 1998), especially her sections on von Balthasar and on Anthony Kelly.

3. Philip J. Rosato, SJ, "Spirit Christology: Ambiguity and Promise," *Theological Studies* 38 (1977): 423–449. He reviews the positions of Walter Kasper and Wolfhart Pannenberg on 438–444 and concludes that they converge on the centrality of the resurrection for Christology but that this should, following Kasper, include a strong recognition of Jesus' union with the Spirit, "his Spirit-filled nature," from the beginning of his existence.

4. Ibid., 445.

5. François-Xavier Durrwell, *Holy Spirit of God: An Essay in Biblical Theology*, trans. Sister Benedict Davies, OSU (London: Geoffrey Chapman, 1986 [French original, 1983]), 146 (italics in original).

6. Ibid., 141 (italics in original).

7. For a historical reading of what Jesus might have originally intended by this parable, see Michael L. Cook, SJ, "Jesus' Parables and the Faith That Does Justice," *Studies in the Spirituality of Jesuits* 24/5 (November 1992): 1–35 In addition, for very helpful insights into the social and cultural context of the parables as peasants would have heard them, see Kenneth E. Bailey, *Poet and Peasant and Through Peasant Eyes. A Literary-Cultural Approach to the Parables in Luke*, Combined Edition (Grand Rapids, MI: Eerdmans, 1983).

8. *Compassion* (*rachamim* in Hebrew) does not mean pity or even sympathy or empathy. Related to the Hebrew word for *womb* (*rechem*), it is the kind of love that a mother has for the child in her womb. If that child is suffering or is threatened in any way the mother will do all she can to alleviate the conditions that cause the suffering or threat. Thus, it is an active virtue. It is worth noting that the father in the parable acts in ways uncharacteristic and unexpected in a patriarchal society. He acts more like a mother than a father.

9. James D. G. Dunn, *Jesus and the Spirit: A Study of the Religious and Charismatic Experience of Jesus and the First Christians as Reflected in the New Testament* (Philadelphia: Westminster Press, 1975), 121 (italics in original). Dunn sees this distinction as Paul's attempt to maintain

the Hebrew notion of bodily resurrection as indicating the whole person while diverting the Hellenistic aversion to material reality onto the flesh. For a more detailed discussion of Paul's anthropological terminology, see James D. G. Dunn, *The Theology of Paul the Apostle* (Grand Rapids, MI: Eerdmans, 1998), 51–78.

10. Unless otherwise noted, biblical translations are from the New Revised Standard Version (NRSV): Michael D. Coogan, ed., *The New Oxford Annotated Bible*, 3rd ed. (New York: Oxford University Press, 2001).

11. James D. G. Dunn, "Jesus—Flesh and Spirit. An Exposition of Romans 1:3–4" in his collected essays, *The Christ & The Spirit*, vol. 1, *Christology* (Grand Rapids, MI: Eerdmans, 1998), 126–153, makes the important point that both the continuity and the difference between the historical and the glorified Jesus was understood in the early Church in terms of Jesus' relation to the Spirit both in his earthly and in his exalted life. He analyzes Rom 1:3–4 primarily but sees the same connection at 1 Tim 3:16 and 1 Pet 3:18. However, the shift from Jesus as a man inspired by the Spirit to Jesus as Lord of the Spirit from the resurrection "installed [or, declared?] Son of God in power according to the Spirit of holiness" at Rom 1:4 led the early Church to "shy away from the unequivocal affirmation that Jesus was raised by the Spirit...although it would appear to be the logical corollary to the twin propositions that the resurrection of Christians will be by the Spirit (Rom 8:11) and that Christ's is the *aparche* of Christians' resurrection (1 Cor 15:20, 44f.)" (152, italics in original). Of course, it is the Father who raised Jesus but the "logical corollary" can hold as a further, and according to Kilian McDonnell necessary, interpretation of the "rich triadic teaching" of the New Testament.

12. According to Dunn, "1 Corinthians 15:45—Last Adam, Life-Giving Spirit" (in ibid., 154–166), Paul can affirm that the risen Christ is a *sōma pneumatikon* (v. 44) because the experiential ground is the communal experience of the risen Christ as "a life-giving spirit" (v. 45). This is what Jesus *became* (*egeneto*) at the moment of his resurrection and what the community hopes to become through the gradual transformation from death into life that the Spirit guarantees (*arrabōn* at 2 Cor 1:21–22; 5:5) but that receives its bodily concretization in the life, death, and resurrection of Jesus. "In short, verse 45b constitutes proof because Paul's experience of the *pneuma zoōpoioun* convinces him that

the exalted Jesus has a spiritual, somatic existence and that in that mode of existence he is the pattern and forerunner of a new humanity" (164).

13.   For a fuller analysis of the historical probabilities, see Michael L. Cook, SJ, *The Jesus of Faith* (New York/Mahwah, NJ: Paulist Press, 1981), 63–72.

14.   Ibid., 100–113. See J. A. T. Robinson, "The Most Primitive Christology of All?" in *Twelve New Testament Studies* (London: SCM Press, 1962), 139–153. Dunn, *The Theology of Paul the Apostle*, 296, comments: "As the formulation of Jesus' vindication in terms of 'resurrection' was an astonishing 'first' in Christian theologizing, so the claim that their vindicated Messiah would come again (to earth) was likewise something hitherto unheard of in the theologizing of Second Temple Judaism."

15.   There were a variety of ways to imagine the coming of God's Kingdom. See Michael L. Cook, SJ, *Justice, Jesus, and the Jews* (Collegeville, MN: Liturgical Press, 2003), 73ff. I refer in n. 3 (p. 101) to Geza Vermes, *Jesus and the World of Judaism* (Philadelphia: Fortress Press, 1983), 32–35, who "outlines four views of the kingdom: (1) YHWH promises power and conquest as king of Israel (Ps 2:8–11; 99:1–3); (2) a royal Messiah will come (*Ps Sol* 17:23–32); (3) apocalyptic victory; (4) the nations will flock to Zion (Isa 60:1–6) with no violence or war. He sees Jesus as favoring the last."

16.   See Dunn, *The Theology of Paul the Apostle*, 298–313.

17.   Martin Hengel, "Christology and New Testament Chronology" in *Between Jesus and Paul* (Philadelphia: Fortress Press, 1983), 30–47. He cautions against over-systematizing the early developments in Christology. "Ancient man did not think analytically or make differentiations within the realm of myth in the way that we do, but combined and accumulated his ideas in a 'multiplicity of approximations'. The more titles were applied to the risen Christ, the more possible it was to celebrate the uniqueness of his saving work". Martin Hengel, *The Son of God* (Philadelphia: Fortress Press, 1976), 57. He says the same in the above article on chronology at 41.

18.   Larry W. Hurtado, *Lord Jesus Christ: Devotion to Jesus in Earliest Christianity* (Grand Rapids, MI: Eerdmans, 2003), 214–216, summarizes his treatment of "Early Pauline Christianity" (79–153) and "Judean Jewish Christianity" (155–216) in reference to his sources: "I have restricted my discussion here to traditions in Paul that may stem

from Judean circles, and to the representations of the Jerusalem church in Acts. These are probably most widely regarded as the data with the strongest claims to being evidence of the beliefs and religious practice of Judean believers" (215). This setting includes both Aramaic-speaking and Greek-speaking believers who on the issue of cultic devotion to Jesus would be in agreement.

19. Hurtado contends "that we need to allow specifically for the causative significance of revelatory experiences in the religious innovations that took place in these circles. That is, I hold that an adequate historical understanding of early Christianity requires us to give significant attention to the religious experiences that obviously formed such a major part of the early Christian ethos" Ibid., 66 (italics in original). He cites Dunn, *Jesus and the Spirit*, 3–4 in support. Dunn speaks of the creative power of Paul's religious experience as an important factor that should not be discounted. Recent articles that relate to this theme include Frank J. Matera, "Christ in the Theologies of Paul and John: Diverse Unity of New Testament Theology," *Theological Studies* 67 (2006): 237–256, who speaks of the "foundational experiences" of Paul and of the Beloved Disciple in John that give shape to their distinct Christologies, and James R. Pambrun, "Revelation and Interiority: The Contribution of Frederick E. Crowe, SJ"(in ibid., 320–344), who seeks to ground revelation in the affective experience of "interiority."

20. Hurtado, commenting on the radical change in Paul and the resultant devotion to Jesus, concludes: "I submit that the most reasonable inference from these things is this: what drew the intense ire of the preconversion Paul against Jewish Christians was not (as has often been alleged, though with scarcely any basis) their supposed laxity of Torah observance or an unseemly association with Gentiles; instead it was the Christ-devotion that is basically reflected in what he embraced and advocated after his conversion. The religious zeal of Saul the Pharisee against Jewish Christians is best accounted for as provoked by what he regarded as their undue reverence of Jesus. They acclaimed a false teacher as Messiah, and may even have seemed to Paul to have compromised Jewish responsibilities to observe the uniqueness of the one God in their devotional practice" *Lord Jesus Christ*, 176.

21. Hurtado (ibid., 101–108) reviews the fifteen references in Paul's seven undisputed letters to "Son," which include only three references to "Son of God." Paul's preferred title to express divinity and

cultic devotion is "Lord." "Son" expresses Jesus' filial relation to God in which we share by adoption.

22. See Cook, *Justice*, 42–46, relying on the insights of Katharine Doob Sakenfeld, *Faithfulness in Action: Loyalty in Biblical Perspective* (Philadelphia: Fortress Press, 1985).

23. Hurtado, *Lord Jesus Christ*, 108–117, analyses the use of "Lord." He comments that in the seven undisputed letters of Paul *Kyrios* is used "about 180 times."

24. This is Hurtado's main point throughout his analysis of the "Pauline evidence" (156–176) regarding cultic devotion to Jesus. He summarizes his view of Paul's connection to early Jewish Christian beliefs and practices on 175. I agree with this but wish to emphasize the inseparable connection of these early experiences with the Holy Spirit.

25. Dunn, *Jesus and the Spirit*, 155. See the similar description at the conclusion of his next chapter on "Enthusiastic Beginning in Lukan Retrospect" (193).

26. Ibid., 350–357. I am employing Dunn's four points but with some modifications.

27. Durrwell, *Holy Spirit of God*, 141 (italics in original). The reference to Irenaeus is *Adversus Omnes Haereses* III, 18, 3.

28. For a fuller account in connection with Mark's Gospel as a whole, see Cook, *Narrative Quest*, 67–108 (chap. 2 on Mark) and 79–81 on the baptism in particular.

29. Dunn, *Jesus and the Spirit*, 11–92. See also James D. G. Dunn, *Christianity in the Making*, Volume 1, *Jesus Remembered* (Grand Rapids, MI: Eerdmans, 2003), 615–762. This volume is an excellent detailed study of the historical Jesus that recognizes an overemphasis in biblical criticism of the Jesus material on literary comparisons with a corresponding neglect of the dynamics of oral tradition. He shows how many of the variations in the Synoptic Gospels can be explained as variations in oral transmission. Frequently, texts may agree on the central point of a story while varying in details. This is not to deny the importance of literary analysis but it does help to clarify a number of apparent anomalies.

30. Joseph A. Fitzmyer, SJ, *The Gospel According to Luke I–IX*, Anchor Bible 28 (New York: Doubleday, 1981), 338. He refers to his agreement with Raymond E. Brown. He also emphasizes the primarily christological intent of the text. "What is involved here is the growing

understanding of the early church about the identity of Jesus. Though at first such titles as Son of God were attached to him primarily as of the resurrection (besides Rom 1:4, see Acts 13:33), the time came when early Christians began to realize that he had to have been such even earlier in his career, even though it had not been recognized. It is not so much that the 'christological moment' (Brown, *Birth*, passim) was pushed back as that there was a growth in awareness as time passed among early Christians that what Jesus was recognized to be after the resurrection he must have been still earlier" (340). See his whole discussion on 337–341, 350–351. The translation "will cast a shadow over" is Fitzmyer's.

31.   For the analysis of the hymn into four strophes, see Raymond E. Brown, SS, *The Gospel According to John I-XII*, Anchor Bible 29 (New York: Doubleday, 1966), 3–37. I offer an analysis of the biblical foundations of the creeds and especially of the six hymns in *Narrative Quest*, 110–116.

32.   James D. G. Dunn, *Christology in the Making: A New Testament Inquiry into the Origins of the Doctrine of the Incarnation* (Philadelphia: Westminster, 1980), 243 (italics in original). The second edition (Grand Rapids, MI: Eerdmans, 1996) is exactly the same except for a long foreword (xi–xxxix) where he replies to his critics. He takes up this and related issues in *The Christ and the Spirit*, Volume 1, *Christology*, 257–314.

33.   Ibid., 212. In the summary of the next chapter on "The Word of God," he emphasizes that the prologue is unique in its identification of the Word of God with a particular person (248–250).

34.   Hurtado, *Lord Jesus Christ*, stresses the importance of Jesus' name as included in early Christian cultic worship that maintains a strong monotheistic faith in the God of Israel. For example, in reference to the Gospel of John, he comments that the author "insists that proper obedience to, and reverence of, God now requires that Jesus be explicitly included with God as recipient of faith and devotion. This means that 'the Father' is now defined with reference to Jesus, through whom in a uniquely full and authoritative measure the Father is revealed" (390).

35.   Ilia Delio, OSF, "Is Creation Eternal?" *Theological Studies* 66 (2005): 279–303 (at 286). On 291 she says: "Creation is an expression of God's desire that [finite] others share in the glory of [infinite] trinitarian love. God's desire for that which God creates means that creation

cannot be in a state of equilibrium or at rest but rather is dynamically oriented toward the triune, God."

36. Pannenberg, *Systematic Theology*, vol. 1, 327–336. Thomas G. Weinandy, OFM Cap., *Does God Change? The Word's Becoming in the Incarnation* (Still River, MA: St. Bede's Publications, 1985) insists on the immutability of God if it is truly God who becomes man. He bases this on the notion of the divine persons as "fully actualized relations" so that becoming man does not entail any new relation but rather the real expression of God's full reality as God, i.e., God is really, not logically, related to creation as God.

37. Delio, "Is Creation Eternal?" 298. See also the analysis of Bonaventure's view in Ilia Delio, OSF, "Theology, Metaphysics, and the Centrality of Christ," *Theological Studies* 68 (2007): 254–273, and her full treatment, *Christ in Evolution* (Maryknoll, NY: Orbis, 2008).

Chapter Three

1. Vladimir Lossky, "Tradition and Traditions" in Daniel B. Clendenin, ed., *Eastern Orthodox Theology: A Contemporary Reader*, 2nd ed. (Grand Rapids, MI: Baker Academic, 2003), 134. Original in Vladimir Lossky, *In the Image and Likeness of God* (Crestwood, NY: St. Vladimir's Seminary Press, 1985), 141–168.

2. Ibid., 135.

3. "...the secret tradition (*dogma*) can be declared publicly and thus become preaching (*kērygma*) when a necessity (for example, the struggle against a heresy) obliges the church to make a pronouncement." Ibid., 129.

4. See chapter 1, nn. 45, 46. This is the opinion of many authors, both East and West. Doctrinally, the normative teaching is the Ecumenical Council, notwithstanding the theological opinion of Augustine and its subsequent use in what Pope Paul VI called the "Western synods" of Lyons (1274) and Florence (1439). It was used at Toledo (589, 633) to counter Arianism (i.e., as an argument for the equality of the Son) as a legitimate variant (interpretation) and was popularized by Pepin and Charlemagne. It was resisted by Pope Leo III in 810 because the liturgical creed should not be amended but was accepted by Pope Benedict VIII in 1014. In the East, Photius advocated *monopatrism* (the Father as the *sole* source of the triune life) but many

Eastern theologians have recognized some role of the Son in the procession of the Spirit. See Corinne Winter, "Filioque" in Richard P. McBrien, ed., *Encyclopedia of Catholicism* (New York: HarperCollins, 1995), 529–530 and Edwards, *Breath of Life*, 145–157. See also André de Halleux, "Towards an Ecumenical Agreement on the Procession of the Holy Spirit and the Addition of the Filioque to the Creed" (in Vischer, *Spirit of God, Spirit of Christ*, 69–84), who sees no obstacle to unity based on the original Creed of Constantinople, which was not concerned with the later question of the relation of Son and Spirit but principally, against the "pneumatomachoi," with the divinity of the Spirit. He also questions the common view above of the addition to the Creed as anti-Arian and suggests it may originally have been "no more than a natural adaptation to the local tradition" (83; see 80–84).

5.   Ware, *The Orthodox Church*, 264–273; Alexander Schmemann, *For the Life of the World: Sacraments and Orthodoxy*, 2nd ed. (Crestwood, NY: St. Vladimir's Seminary Press, 1973), 23–46.

6.   Schmemann, *For the Life*, 34.

7.   Ibid., 27. The summary of the experience is taken mostly from Schmemann.

8.   Leonid Ouspensky, "The Meaning and Content of the Icon" in Clendenin, *Eastern Orthodox Theology*, 35. The article is from Leonid Ouspensky, *Theology of the Icon*, trans. Anthony Gythiel and Elizabeth Meyendorff, 2 vols. (Crestwood, NY: St. Vladimir's Seminary Press, 1992), 1:151–194.

9.   Ibid., 40.

10.   Aristotle Papanikolaou, "Divine Energies or Divine Personhood: Vladimir Lossky and John Zizioulas on Conceiving the Transcendent and Immanent God," *Modern Theology* 19 (2003): 371. In an earlier article, Lucian Turcescu offers a rather trenchant criticism of Zizioulas' interpretation of the Greek Fathers: "'Person' Versus 'Individual', and Other Modern Misreadings of Gregory of Nyssa," *Modern Theology* 18 (2002): 527–539. Papanikolaou comments: "The many detractors of Zizioulas's interpretation of the Greek fathers notwithstanding, what is suggestive about Zizioulas's theology is his claim that *hypostasis* both in its trinitarian and christological developments must imply more than simply identifying the fact of irreducible distinctions in God, or the means for uniting divine and human natures. *Hypostasis* is that in and through which divine-human communion is

realized, and is a distinction necessary not simply for conceptualizing how such a communion is possible *in* Christ, but how it is possible at all. In this sense, Zizioulas's 'ontology', though not explicit in the Greek fathers, may be interpreted to be consistent with their own logic" ibid., 378 (italics in original). For the purposes of this book, I would affirm Zizioulas's appeal to a "neopatristic synthesis" (*Being as Communion*, 26) that seeks the common roots of both East and West. In the light of Papanikolaou's comment, the question can further be asked: does tradition allow for a contemporary understanding of person that includes but transcends the particular context and concerns of the Church Fathers, such as the Cappadocians?

11. Papanikolaou, "Divine Energies," 359.

12. Vladimir Lossky, "Apophasis and Trinitarian Theology" in Clendinin, *Eastern Orthodox Theology*, 162. Original in Lossky, *Image and Likeness*, 13–29.

13. Vladimir Lossky, "The Procession of the Holy Spirit in Orthodox Trinitarian Theology" in Clendinen, *Eastern Orthodox Theology*, 170. Original in Lossky, *Image and Likeness*, 71–96. See the summary of Lossky's "antinomic theology" in relation to the *filioque* in Papanikolaou, "Divine Energies," 360–363. We will return to Lossky's view on the *filioque* below.

14. Papanikolaou, "Divine Energies," 375.

15. Ibid., 375 (italics in original).

16. Ibid., 373. "The crucial difference between Lossky and Zizioulas is that the latter is making a claim that God in *theologia* is knowable, though not exhaustively so, and it is this knowledge which forms the condition for the possibility of expressing theologically a trinitarian ontology of personhood" Ibid., 374. My summary of these views is clearly indebted to Papanikolaou's fine article and to his many references to the two authors. For a fuller account of the views of Lossky and Zizioulas, with abundant references and bibliography, see Aristotle Papanikolaou, *Being With God: Trinity, Apophaticism, and Divine-Human Communion* (Notre Dame, IN: University of Notre Dame Press, 2006).

17. Zizioulas, *Being as Communion*, 16–17.

18. Ibid., 17–18 (italics in original).

19. Ibid, 41. On 39–41, he develops the two "leavenings." In n. 34, he refers to Rahner's critique of the typically Western approach of starting with the one God and then moving to the Trinity. See Karl

Rahner, *The Trinity*, trans. Joseph Donceel (New York: Herder & Herder, 1970).

20. Ibid., 49.

21. Ibid., 55, n. 49 (italics in original).

22. Ibid., 101–109.

23. Ibid., 130.

24. Ibid., 172–188, for his discussion of the two approaches and their synthesis in the Eucharist.

25. Ibid., 118.

26. "...Zizioulas is correct in thinking that *hypostasis* is the category through which to think divine-human communion, especially if such a communion is to be trinitarian, i.e., *in* Christ. The language of hypostasis allows for a conceptualization of the realism of such a divine-human communion in a way not open to language of essence or of *hyper*-essence." Papanikolaou, "Divine Energies," 378 (italics in original).

27. Lossky, "The Procession," 163.

28. Ibid., 169 (italics in original).

29. Ibid., 171. Quote is from Gregory Nazianzus, *Orationes*, 31.14.

30. Ibid., 179–180. In an essay that confirms many of Lossky's views among the Greek Fathers, Markos Orphanos comments: "The Greek Fathers were also cautious and rejected the Latins' conclusion that the 'order' of manifestation and names of the divine Prosopa implies their existential and natural order as well. For the Greeks there is no ontological order whatsoever in the Holy Trinity." Markos A. Orphanos, "The Procession of the Holy Spirit According to Certain Later Greek Fathers" in Vischer, *Spirit of God, Spirit of Christ*, 44.

31. Boris Bobrinskoy, "The Filioque Yesterday and Today" in Vischer, *Spirit of God, Spirit of Christ*, 144.

32. Thomas Smail, "The Holy Spirit in the Holy Trinity" in Christopher R. Seitz, ed., *Nicene Christianity: The Future for a New Ecumenism* (Grand Rapids, MI: Brazos Press, 2001), 164 (italics in original).

33. Jürgen Moltmann, *The Way of Jesus Christ: Christology in Messianic Dimensions*, trans. Margaret Kohl (New York: HarperCollins, 1990), 297. See my review in *Horizons* 19 (Spring 1992): 141–142.

34. Pannenberg, *Systematic Theology*, vol. 1, 410.

35. "To formulate conditions for consistent talk about God in general, however, is not to describe the concrete reality of God with

the essential attributes which come to light in his specific acts in history." Ibid., 394.

36. Ibid., 447.

37. Peters, *God as Trinity*, 168. He offers a clear and helpful review of the issues of time and eternity both for science and for theology in chapter 4, "The Temporal and Eternal Trinity," 146–187.

38. Ibid., 170.

Chapter Four

1. Kasper, *The God of Jesus Christ*, 289. See 285–290 for his discussion of the language of three persons.

2. Ibid., 290, referring to the views of Joseph Ratzinger. On 307, he affirms the Trinity as communion: "Communion is thus a union of persons and at the same time maintains the primacy of the always unique person." On 281–282, he explains the term *subsistent relations* in contrast to the Anselmian sense of "the foundation of the subsistence." Rather, with Eastern trinitarian thinking, he sees the persons "as grounding the relations." Hence, the persons are "logically prior to the relations."

3. Ibid., 222.

4. Ibid., 316. In his concluding remarks commenting on the doctrine of the Trinity in the light of John 17 (303–309), he remarks: "The intention of the trinitarian confession is thus not really a teaching about God but the doxology or eschatological glorification of God. The doctrine of the Trinity is as it were simply the grammar of the doxology....The doctrine of the Trinity acquires its meaning from the unity-in-tension of doxology and soteriology. There is no need to choose between the approaches of Karl Barth and Karl Rahner" (304).

5. "The doctrine of the Trinity has become important in the last ten years because it is the way in which the distinctive feature of Christianity is formulated. Dialogue with other religions is not helped if Christians relativize that which is distinctively Christian and give it up in favour of a general pluralism. Who would be interested in a dialogue with Christian theologians who no longer want to advocate Christianity clearly?" Jürgen Moltmann, *History and the Triune God: Contributions to Trinitarian Theology*, trans. John Bowden (New York: Crossroad, 1992), xi. In the preface, he says that this collection of articles was written in

the years 1980–1990 as a further interpretation of his "social doctrine of the Trinity" developed in his 1980 book, *The Trinity and the Kingdom of God*, trans. Margaret Kohl (London: SCM Press, 1981). In Part 3, "My Theological Career" (165–182), he describes his experiences of World War II and comments: "What can one talk about after Auschwitz if not about God?" (166). He refers to his "methods" in three respects: (1) "The whole of theology in one focal point," which includes *The Theology of Hope* (1964), *The Crucified God* (1972), and *The Church in the Power of the Spirit* (1975). (2) "Theology in movement, dialogue and conflict," which embraces a wide variety of experiences in dialogue with the other. (3) "The part as a contribution to the whole," which includes *The Trinity and the Kingdom of God* (1980) and his further work on pneumatology: *The Spirit of Life* (1991) and many other works, e.g., *Science and Wisdom* (2002). Given his enormous productivity, we will concentrate on his later "contributions," especially the works on the Trinity, for the purposes of this book.

6.   Moltmann, *History and the Triune God*, xiii. He refers here to a book by Bernd Jochen Hilberath. See the latter's article, "Identity Through Self-Transcendence" in Hinze and Dabney, *Advents*, 265–294, as referred to above in the introduction.

7.   Ibid., xvi. He develops this in *The Trinity and the Kingdom*, "II. The Passion of God," 21–60. "If we follow through the idea that the historical passion of Christ reveals the eternal passion of God, then the self-sacrifice of love is God's eternal nature" (32).

8.   Moltmann, "The Trinitarian Personhood of the Holy Spirit" in Hinze and Dabney, *Advents*, 303. The following sentences of this paragraph have already been cited in our introduction.

9.   Moltmann, *History and the Triune God*, 80–89. "In the life of the immanent Trinity everything is unique.…In the doctrine of the immanent Trinity we may basically only narrate, and not subsume. We have to remain concrete, since, as history shows, heresies lurk in abstractions. By contrast, the foundation of orthodoxy lies in narrative differentiation" (89). See also *The Trinity and the Kingdom*, 188–190.

10.   Moltmann, *The Trinity and the Kingdom*, 19.

11.   Ibid., 125.

12.   Ibid., 53 (italics in original). See his comments in the next section on "God is love" (57–60). In trinitarian terms: "Creation is a part of the eternal love affair between the Father and the Son. It springs

from the Father's love for the Son and is redeemed by the answering love of the Son for the Father. Creation exists because the eternal love communicates himself creatively to his Other. It exists because the eternal love seeks fellowship and desires response in freedom. That is why we have indeed to see the history of creation as *the tragedy of the divine love*, but must view the history of redemption as *the feast of the divine joy*" (59, italics in original).

13. Ibid., 142 (italics mine).

14. Ibid., 149 (italics in original).

15. Ibid., 150.

16. Ibid., 153. God's fidelity and reliability yield the following principle for trinitarian doctrine: "Statements about the immanent Trinity must not contradict statements about the economic Trinity. Statements about the economic Trinity must correspond to doxological statements about the immanent Trinity" ibid., 154 (italics in original). For the affirmation of Rahner's axiom, see 160.

17. Moltmann, "The Trinitarian Personhood of the Holy Spirit" in Hinze and Dabney, *Advents*, 309. This article is a reprise and development of his earlier treatment in *The Spirit of Life*, 268–309. Also, he summarizes his view on doxology in *History and the Triune God*, 68–69, and states that in the monarchical and eucharistic forms of the Trinity the Spirit appears to be subordinated to the Father and Son. While worship and glorification stem from the experiences of salvation and thanksgiving, they go beyond them in focusing on God for God's own sake, the vision of the eternal fellowship of the Spirit with the Father and Son. "In this doxology of God for God's sake, all trinitarian pneumatology finds its fulfillment" (69).

18. Moltmann, "The Trinitarian Personhood of the Holy Spirit" in Hinze and Dabney, *Advents*, 310.

19. Moltmann, "Theological Proposals Towards the Resolution of the Filioque Controversy" in Vischer, *Spirit of God, Spirit of Christ*, 171 (italics in original).

20. Ibid., 167, 168, 169.

21. Moltmann, *The Trinity and the Kingdom*, 157.

22. Moltmann, "The Trinitarian Personhood of the Holy Spirit" in Hinze and Dabney, *Advents*, 313 (italics in original).

23. Ibid., 312–313. Note that this contrasts with Coffey's insistence that there can be no additional names other than the traditional

names of Father-Son-Spirit in, among other places, "Spirit Christology and the Trinity" (in ibid., 333–334). Moltmann sees different roles in relation to each other, whereas Coffey sees the proper role of each in the constitution of the persons.

24. Moltmann, *The Trinity and the Kingdom*, 184.

25. See the comments of Vladimir Lossky and Markos Orphanos in chapter 3 of our text.

26. In *The Spirit of Life*, 306–309, he states clearly the simultaneity of the begetting and the procession: "In the eternal simultaneity of the Trinity, the begetting of the Son does not take priority over the procession of the Spirit. The Orthodox theologians are right when they talk about a reciprocal 'accompaniment'—the Spirit accompanies the begetting of the Son, and the Son accompanies the procession of the Spirit. They are then admittedly changing the metaphor for the Trinity and are no longer talking about the Son and the Spirit, but about God's Word and his Breath" (307). Employing the metaphors of "Word" and "Breath," he affirms that the Father "utters" the Word and "breathes forth" the Spirit simultaneously. In accord with the Orthodox view, he develops the images of the Spirit as *accompanying* (manifestation), so that the Son is begotten *through* the Spirit, of *resting* (dwelling place), so that the Son is begotten as the eternal dwelling place of the Spirit, and of *shining* (light/glory), so that the Son is begotten as the source of eternal light that illumines the mutual relations of Father and Son, giving them eternal joy and eternal bliss. He sees these three images of "accompanies," "rests," and "shines" as corresponding better to "the Spirit-history of Christ" and "the Christ-history of the Spirit" in the New Testament. This reciprocal relationship between Son and Spirit is "the most important theological objection to the Filioque" (308).

27. Del Colle, *Christ and the Spirit*, 95. In chapter 4, entitled "Beyond Neo-scholasticism: The Spirit-christology of David Coffey" (91–140), Del Colle offers an extensive and sympathetic review of Coffey's work and its development. He points out that initially Coffey used a "bestowal model" but later preferred a "return model" ("mutual love") to move beyond neo-scholasticism (96–97).

28. Coffey, "Spirit Christology and the Trinity" in Hinze and Dabney, *Advents*, 323.

29. Coffey, *Deus Trinitas*, 155.

30. Ibid., 32. See also the citations from our introduction.

31. Ibid., 45.

32. Ibid., 34.

33. Ibid., 35.

34. See also Ralph Del Colle, "The Holy Spirit: Presence, Power, Person," *Theological Studies* 62 (2001): 322–340, who argues that the experience of the Spirit as person is grounded in our experience of human transformation. Also, in his "Response to Jürgen Moltmann and David Coffey" in Hinze and Dabney, *Advents*, 339–346, he comments: "…the Spirit is fully personal when given, in this case, by the Father and the Son in the Pentecostal sending creating a community of persons-in-relation, analogous to the relationality recognized between Father and Son in another, the person of the Holy Spirit" (344).

35. Coffey, *Deus Trinitas*, 41

36. David M. Coffey, "A Proper Mission of the Holy Spirit," *Theological Studies* 47 (1986): 227–250. "The Holy Spirit enters the plan of salvation through his personal action at the beginning of Jesus' life, making him Son of God in humanity. He enters upon his proper mission as sent by Christ at the end of that life, having become in the course of it fully 'incarnate' in Jesus' love of God and neighbor. Christ sends him into the world in that through his death and resurrection he pours out in power on his brethren his love for them" (239). In my presentation of Coffey's views, I am relying primarily on *Deus Trinitas* and his article in *Advents*. However, he has written a number of other articles to expand and develop his views, most notably a series in *Theological Studies* (*TS*): "The 'Incarnation' of the Holy Spirit in Christ," *TS* 45 (1984): 466–480; *TS* 47 (cited above); "The Holy Spirit as the Mutual Love of the Father and the Son," *TS* 51 (1990): 193–229; "The Theandric Nature of Christ," *TS* 60 (1999): 405–431; "Response to Neil Ormerod, and Beyond," *TS* 68 (2007): 900–915; "A Trinitarian Response to Issues Raised by Peter Phan," *TS* 69 (2008): 852–874.

37. Coffey, *Deus Trinitas*, 50–51 (italics in original).

38. Ibid., 51. He also makes use of this distinction in his article in *Advents*, 330–333.

39. Ibid., 49, n. 7 (163–164). This is a long note in response to Thomas Weinandy's view that the passivity of the Holy Spirit is "hardly compatible with his being a person." He also addresses Weinandy's view in his article in *Advents*, (334–335). We will return to this.

40. Ibid., 52–53 (italics in original).

41.   Ibid., 50, citing Moltmann, "Theological Proposals" in Vischer, *Spirit of God, Spirit of Christ*, 169. Coffey disagrees because for him what the Spirit receives from the Son is the Son's love of the Father that constitutes the Spirit as the mutual love of Father and Son. In a chapter entitled "Recent Theology: Moltmann" (105–130), he offers an extensive review of Moltmann's work, especially his focus on the cross. Along with the other "Paschal Mystery theologians" he treats (Juengel, Muehlen, and von Balthasar), he contrasts his theology of coming to the cross as the climax of Jesus' life and ministry with their exclusive concentration on the cross. All agree, however, that access to the doctrine of the Trinity is through "the trinitarian structure of salvation in Christ," which is primarily dependent on the biblical data (148–150).

42.   Ibid., 58.

43.   In his article "The Theandric Nature of Christ," Coffey argues, in the light of his Spirit Christology, that Christ's love for the Father and for us "is identical with the person of the Holy Spirit, divine love incarnate in human love" (426, referring to his earlier article, "The 'Incarnation' of the Holy Spirit in Christ").

44.   Coffey, *Deus Trinitas*, 60–65.

45.   Moltmann, "Theological Proposals" in Vischer, *Spirit of God, Spirit of Christ*, 172–173.

46.   Del Colle, "Response" in Hinze and Dabney, *Advents*, pinpoints this: "Yet we are still confronted by the 'how' of this reciprocity. The answer, I suggest, lies in how the Holy Spirit is person, that is, constituted person by the originary hypostatic relations" (344).

47.   Coffey, *Deus Trinitas*, 148, summarizes his view and responds to Weinandy in n. 75 (183). This interpretation of Luke 1:35 is foundational to his development of the return model and he treats it in many places, e.g., in his article "The Theandric Nature of Christ" (425 ff). He sees his view as corresponding to his ascending Spirit Christology that complements and completes a descending Logos Christology. Weinandy, for his part, while affirming that the union of incarnation must precede sanctification by the Spirit, certainly affirms the creative activity of the Spirit at the conception but in concert with the Father in a trinitarian pattern: "The depiction of the Father begetting his Son in the womb of Mary by the Holy Spirit becomes, I believe, a temporal icon of his eternally begetting the Son by the Holy Spirit." Thomas G. Weinandy, OFM Cap., *The Father's Spirit of Sonship: Reconceiving the Trinity* (Edinburgh: T&T Clark, 1995), 42.

48. Weinandy, *The Father's Spirit of Sonship*, 97–98.

49. Ibid., 78–79.

50. Ibid., ix. He states the thesis more fully on 17–18.

51. Ibid., 14–15. In n. 28, he emphasizes that this is "one act of being interrelated."

52. Ibid., 54.

53. Ibid., 59, citing Thomas Aquinas, *Summa Theologica*, 1, 39, 1.

54. Ibid., 60.

55. Ibid., 64. He credits Athanasius over against the later Cappadocians as having the true insight into the import of the *homoousios* that shatters the Platonic principle of emanation represented by the tendency to replace it with *homoiousios*. See ibid., 11–13 and n. 26 where he cites David Coffey and T. F. Torrance as well as his own work: *Does God Change? The Word's Becoming in the Incarnation*, 10–16.

56. Ibid., 66.

57. Ibid., 69. Moltmann addresses this same question in "The Trinitarian Personhood of the Holy Spirit" in Hinze and Dabney, *Advents*, 313, by emphasizing that each person has a different relationship to the other two.

58. Ibid., 69. Commenting on Durrwell's view that the Spirit *is* the begetting, he distinguishes begetting and proceeding. "I would want to say that the Spirit proceeds from the Father in the begetting of the Son and that the Son is begotten in or by the Spirit. The begetting and the spirating are simultaneous but distinct acts of the Father" (71, n. 32).

59. Ibid., 72.

60. Ibid., 82–83.

61. Coffey, *Deus Trinitas*, n. 7 (163–164) and "Spirit Christology and the Trinity" in Hinze and Dabney, *Advents*, 334–335.

62. Coffey, "Spirit Christology and the Trinity" in Hinze and Dabney, *Advents*, 335.

63. Weinandy, *The Father's Spirit of Sonship*, 100.

Bibliography

Note: When articles cited in the footnotes are parts of collections, only the collections are included in the bibliography.

Bailey, Kenneth E. *Poet and Peasant and Through Peasant Eyes: A Literary-Cultural Approach to the Parables in Luke.* Combined Edition. Grand Rapids, MI: Eerdmans, 1983.

Brown, Raymond E. *The Gospel According to John I–XII.* Anchor Bible 29. New York: Doubleday, 1966.

Clendenin, Daniel B., ed. *Eastern Orthodox Theology: A Contemporary Reader.* 2nd ed. Grand Rapids, MI: Baker Academic, 2003.

Coffey, David M. "A Trinitarian Response to Issues Raised by Peter Phan," *Theological Studies* 69 (2008): 852–874.

————. "Response to Neil Ormerod, and Beyond," *Theological Studies* 68 (2007): 900–915.

————. *Deus Trinitas: The Doctrine of the Triune God.* New York: Oxford University Press, 1999.

———— "The Theandric Nature of Christ," *Theological Studies* 60 (1999): 405–431.

————. "The Holy Spirit as the Mutual Love of the Father and the Son," *Theological Studies* 51 (1990): 193–229.

———— "A Proper Mission of the Holy Spirit," *Theological Studies* 47 (1986): 227–250.

————. "The 'Incarnation' of the Holy Spirit in Christ," *Theological Studies* 45 (1984): 466–480.

Coogan, Michael D., ed. *The New Oxford Annotated Bible.* Third edition. New York: Oxford University Press, 2001.

Cook, Michael L. *Justice, Jesus, and the Jews.* Collegeville, MN: Liturgical Press, 2003.

————. *Christology as Narrative Quest.* Collegeville, MN: Liturgical Press, 1997.

————. "Jesus' Parables and the Faith That Does Justice," *Studies in the Spirituality of Jesuits* 24/5 (1992): 1–35.

————. *The Jesus of Faith: A Study in Christology.* New York/Mahwah, NJ: Paulist Press, 1981.

Cooke, Bernard. *Power and the Spirit of God: Toward an Experience-Based Pneumatology.* New York: Oxford University Press, 2004.

Davies, Paul. *The Mind of God: The Scientific Basis for a Rational World.* New York: Simon & Schuster, 1992.

Del Colle, Ralph. *Christ and the Spirit: Spirit-Christology in Trinitarian Perspective.* New York: Oxford University Press, 1994.

————. "The Holy Spirit: Presence, Power, Person," *Theological Studies* 62 (2001): 322–340.

Delio, Ilia. *Christ in Evolution.* Maryknoll, NY: Orbis, 2008.

————. "Theology, Metaphysics, and the Centrality of Christ," *Theological Studies* 68 (2007): 254–273.

————. "Is Creation Eternal?" *Theological Studies* 66 (2005): 279–303.

Douglass, James W. *Resistance and Contemplation.* New York: Dell, 1972.

Dunn, James D. G. *Christianity in the Making.* Vol. 1. *Jesus Remembered.* Grand Rapids, MI: Eerdmans, 2003.

————. *The Christ & the Spirit.* Vol. 1. *Christology.* Grand Rapids, MI: Eerdmans, 1998.

————. *The Theology of Paul the Apostle.* Grand Rapids, MI: Eerdmans, 1998.

————. *Christology in the Making: A New Testament Inquiry into the Origins of the Doctrine of the Incarnation.* Philadelphia: Westminster Press, 1980.

————. *Jesus and the Spirit: A Study of the Religious and Charismatic Experience of Jesus and the First Christians as Reflected in the New Testament.* Philadelphia: Westminster Press, 1975.

Durrwell, François-Xavier. *Holy Spirit of God: An Essay in Biblical Theology.* Translated by Sister Benedict Davies. London: Geoffrey Chapman, 1986 (from French original of 1983).

Edwards, Denis. *Breath of Life: A Theology of the Creator Spirit.* Maryknoll, NY: Orbis, 2004.

Fitzmyer, Joseph A. *The Gospel According to Luke I-IX.* Anchor Bible 28. New York: Doubleday, 1981.

Bibliography

Fox, Thomas C. *Pentecost in Asia: A New Way of Being Church*. Mary-knoll, NY: Orbis, 2004.

Fries, Paul R., and Tiran Nersoyan, eds. *Christ in East and West*. Macon, GA: Mercer University Press, 1987.

Haight, Roger. "The Case for Spirit Christology," *Theological Studies* 53 (1992): 257–287.

————. *Jesus Symbol of God*. Maryknoll, NY: Orbis, 1999.

Haught, John F. "Darwin, Design, and the Promise of Nature," The Boyle Lecture of February 4, 2004.

————. *Deeper Than Darwin. The Prospect for Religion in the Age of Evolution*. Boulder, CO: Westview Press, 2003.

————. *Responses to 101 Questions on God and Evolution*. New York/Mahwah, NJ: Paulist Press, 2001.

————. *God after Darwin: A Theology of Evolution*. Boulder, CO: Westview Press, 2000.

Hawking, Stephen W. *A Brief History of Time*. New York: Bantam Books, 1988.

Hengel, Martin. *Between Jesus and Paul*. Philadelphia: Fortress Press, 1983.

————. *The Son of God*. Philadelphia: Fortress Press, 1976.

Hinze, Bradford E., and Lyle D. Dabney, eds. *Advents of the Spirit. An Introduction to the Current Study of Pneumatology*. Milwaukee: Marquette University Press, 2001.

Huizing, Peter, and William Bassett, eds. *Experience of the Spirit*. Concilium vol. 9, no. 10. New York: The Seabury Press, 1974.

Hunt, Anne. *Trinity. Nexus of the Mysteries of Christian Faith*. Maryknoll, NY: Orbis, 2005.

————. "Psychological Analogy and Paschal Mystery in Trinitarian Theology," *Theological Studies* 59 (1998): 197–218.

————. *What Are They Saying About the Trinity?* New York/Mahwah, NJ: Paulist Press, 1998.

Hurtado, Larry W. *Lord Jesus Christ: Devotion to Jesus in Earliest Christianity*. Grand Rapids, MI: Eerdmans, 2003.

Johnson, Elizabeth A. *She Who Is. The Mystery of God in Feminist Theological Discourse*. New York: Crossroad, 1992.

Kasper, Walter. *The God of Jesus Christ*. Translated by Matthew J. O'Connell. New York: Crossroad, 1986.

Küng, Hans, and Jürgen Moltmann, eds. *Conflicts About the Holy Spirit.* Concilium 128. New York: Seabury Press, 1979.

LaCugna, Catherine. *God for Us. The Trinity and Christian Life.* New York: HarperSanFrancisco, 1991.

Lossky, Vladimir. *In the Image and Likeness of God.* Crestwood, NY: St. Vladimir's Seminary Press, 1985.

————. *The Mystical Theology of the Eastern Church.* Cambridge and London: James Clarke & Co., 1957 (from French original of 1944).

Matera, Frank J. "Christ in the Theologies of Paul and John: Diverse Unity of New Testament Theology," *Theological Studies* 67 (2006): 237–256.

McDonnell, Kilian. "Theological Presuppositions in Our Preaching about the Spirit," *Theological Studies* 59 (1998): 219–235.

————. "A Trinitarian Theology of the Holy Spirit," *Theological Studies* 46 (1985): 191–227.

Meyendorff, John. *Christ in Eastern Christian Thought.* Washington, DC: Corpus Books, 1969.

Moltmann, Jürgen. *History and the Triune God: Contributions to Trinitarian Theology.* Translated by John Bowden. New York: Crossroad, 1992.

————. *The Spirit of Life: A Universal Affirmation.* Translated by Margaret Kohl. Minneapolis: Fortress Press, 1992.

————. *The Way of Jesus Christ: Christology in Messianic Dimensions.* Translated by Margaret Kohl. New York: HarperCollins, 1990.

————. *The Trinity and the Kingdom of God.* Translated by Margaret Kohl. London: SCM Press, 1981.

O'Murchú, Diarmuid. *Evolutionary Faith: Rediscovering God in Our Great Story.* Maryknoll, NY: Orbis, 2002.

————. *Quantum Theology: Spiritual Implications of the New Physics.* New York: Crossroad, 1997.

Ormerod, Neil. "A Dialectic Engagement with the Social Sciences in an Ecclesiological Context," *Theological Studies* 66 (2005): 815–840.

Ouspensky, Leonid. *Theology of the Icon.* Translated by Anthony Gythiel and Elizabeth Meyendorff. 2 vols. Crestwood, NY: St. Vladimir's Seminary Press, 1992.

Pambrun, James R. "Revelation and Interiority: The Contribution of Frederick E. Crowe, SJ," *Theological Studies* 67 (2006): 320–344.

Pannenberg, Wolfhart. *Systematic Theology*. Vol. 1. Translated by Geoffrey W. Bromiley. Grand Rapids, MI: Eerdmans, 1991.

Papanikolaou, Aristotle. *Being With God: Trinity, Apophaticism, and Divine-Human Communion*. Notre Dame, IN: University of Notre Dame Press, 2006.

————. "Divine Energies or Divine Personhood: Vladimir Lossky and John Zizioulas on Conceiving the Transcendent and Immanent God," *Modern Theology* 19 (2003): 357–385.

Peters, Ted. *God as Trinity: Relationality and Temporality in Divine Life*. Louisville: Westminster/John Knox, 1993.

Phan, Peter C. *Being Religious Interreligiously: Asian Perspectives on Interreligious Dialogue*. Maryknoll, NY: Orbis, 2004.

Polkinghorne, John, ed. *The Work of Love: Creation as Kenosis*. Grand Rapids, MI: Eerdmans, 2001.

Rahner, Karl. *The Trinity*. Translated by Joseph Donceel. New York: Herder & Herder, 1970.

Robinson, J. A. T. *Twelve New Testament Studies*. London: SCM Press, 1962.

Rosato, Philip J. "Spirit Christology: Ambiguity and Promise," *Theological Studies* 38 (1977): 423–449.

Sakenfeld, Katharine Doob. *Faithfulness in Action: Loyalty in Biblical Perspective*. Philadelphia: Fortress Press, 1985.

Schmemann, Alexander. *For the Life of the World: Sacraments and Orthodoxy*. 2nd ed. Crestwood, NY: St. Vladimir's Seminary Press, 1973.

Schnackenburg, Rudolf. *Ephesians: A Commentary*. Translated by Helen Heron. Edinburgh: T&T Clark, 1991.

Seitz, Christopher R., ed. *Nicene Christianity: The Future for a New Ecumenism*. Grand Rapids, MI: Brazos Press, 2001.

Turcescu, Lucian. " 'Person' Versus 'Individual', and Other Modern Misreadings of Gregory of Nyssa," *Modern Theology* 18 (2002): 527–539.

Van Till, Howard J. "The Creation: Intelligently Designed or Optimally Equipped?" *Theology Today* 55 (1998): 344–364.

Vermes, Geza. *Jesus and the World of Judaism*. Philadelphia: Fortress Press, 1983.

Vischer, Lucas, ed. *Spirit of God, Spirit of Christ: Ecumenical Reflections on the Filioque Controversy*. Faith & Order Paper 103. London: SPCK, 1981.

Ware, Timothy. *The Orthodox Church*. London: Penguin Books, 1997.

Weinandy, Thomas G. *Does God Change? The Word's Becoming in the Incarnation*. Still River, MA: St. Bede's Publications, 1985.

————: *The Father's Spirit of Sonship: Reconceiving the Trinity*. Edinburgh: T&T Clark, 1995.

Wink, Walter. *The Human Being: Jesus and the Enigma of the Son of the Man*. Minneapolis: Fortress Press, 2002.

Winter, Corinne. "Filioque" in Richard P. McBrien, ed., *Encyclopedia of Catholicism*. New York: HarperCollins, 1995.

Wright, John H. "Roger Haight's Spirit Christology," *Theological Studies* 53 (1992): 729–735.

Zizioulas, John D., *Being as Communion: Studies in Personhood and the Church*. Crestwood, NY: St. Vladimir's Seminary Press, 1985.